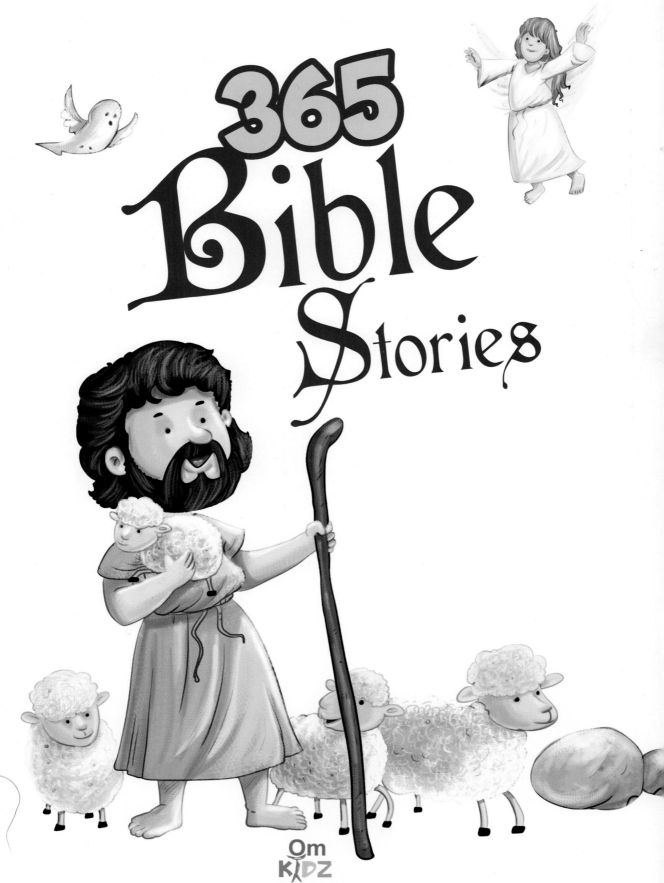

365 Bible Stories

Om KIDZ

An imprint of Om Books International

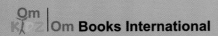 Om Books International

Reprinted in 2019

Corporate & Editorial Office
A-12, Sector 64, Noida 201 301
Uttar Pradesh, India
Phone: +91 120 477 4100
Email: editorial@ombooks.com
Website: www.ombooksinternational.com

Sales Office
107, Ansari Road, Darya Ganj
New Delhi 110 002, India
Phone: +91 11 4000 9000
Email: sales@ombooks.com
Website: www.ombooks.com

Contents

THE OLD TESTAMENT

THE NEW TESTAMENT

AUGUST

SEPTEMBER

OCTOBER

THE OLD
TESTAMENT

01 Introducing the Bible

The Bible is the holy book of the Christian faith, of the followers of Lord Jesus Christ. It is believed that on reading the Bible, one can understand and gain wisdom to live one's life.

The Bible contains stories about the creation of the universe, origin of mankind, beginning of sin and suffering. It also has the story of Jesus and his teachings. All these stories have fascinated readers and believers for many generations.

The Bible can be divided in two parts—the Old Testament and the New Testament ('testament' means agreement). The Old Testament refers to the thirty-nine canonical books of the Hebrew Scriptures written before the coming of Jesus. The New Testament refers to twenty-seven books originally written in Greek by the disciples of Jesus, where they recorded the life of Jesus, His teachings, His miracles and the spread of Christianity.

02 The Creation of Light and Sky

In the beginning, before God created the Universe, the Earth was formless and desolate. The ocean that covered everything was engulfed in darkness. The power of God moved over the ocean.

Then, God commanded, "Let there be light."

And there was light.

God divided the darkness and the light. Then He called the light, 'Day' and the darkness 'Night'. Evening passed and morning came—that was the first day.

The next day, God commanded, "Let there be a dome to divide the water and keep it in two separate places," and He named it 'Sky'.

Evening passed and morning came—that was the second day.

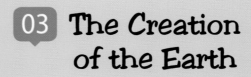

03 The Creation of the Earth

After God created night and day, seas and sky, He was pleased with His creations. Next, God commanded, "Let the water come in one place so that land can appear." He named the land 'Earth' and the water 'Sea'. He then commanded, "Let the Earth produce plants of every kind—those that bear grain and those that bear fruit."

So the Earth produced all kinds of plants and trees, making the Earth very beautiful. Evening passed and morning came—that was the third day. Then, God commanded again, "Let the light in the sky help to separate the day and the night."

Thus, He made the Sun to rule over the day and the Moon to rule over the night. He also made the stars. Everything was good in every way. Evening passed and morning came—that was the fourth day.

04 The Creation of Creatures

On the fifth day, God said, "Let the waters be filled with living beings and let the air be thronged with birds." Evening passed and morning came—that was the fifth day. The next day, God spoke, "Let there be all kinds of animals on Earth."

The whole world was now alive. Finally, God commanded, "Let there be human beings." He made 'Man' in his own image. Then, He made 'Woman' from the Man's rib. He told them, "I have provided everything for your sustenance. Use my creations judiciously."

Evening passed and morning came—that was the sixth day. God took six days to make everything. He rested on the seventh day and blessed the day. He set it apart as a special day because he had completed his creations.

05 The Garden of Eden

God made Man from the dust of the Earth and breathed life-giving breath into his nostrils. That is how the life of Adam started, who was the very first Man.

Then, God made a lovely garden called Eden. It was very considered to be the most beautiful garden; full of trees that bore fruits, decorated lavishly with flowers and streams flowed through it. In the middle of the garden, stood the 'Tree of Knowledge and Life'.

God asked Adam to cultivate and look after the garden and warned, "Do not eat the fruit from the Tree of Knowledge and Life."

06 Adam and Eve

After some time of living in Eden, Adam felt lonely. God thought, "I shall make a suitable companion for him."

So God put Adam into a deep sleep. He removed one rib from Adam's chest and closed up the flesh. He made a woman out of the rib.

When Adam saw her, he knew he had found a true companion.

"Here at last is one of my own kind; bone of my bone and flesh of my flesh."

Adam loved her and named her Eve, meaning 'Mother of all living things'.

07 The First Sin

There was a cunning serpent in the Garden of Eden, he encouraged Eve to eat the fruit from the Tree of Knowledge and Life. Eve did so and shared the fruit with Adam as well. Immediately, they were conscious of their unclothed state and covered themselves with fig leaves.

God called out to them, but they hid in fear.

God asked them, "Did you eat the fruits from the Tree of Knowledge and Life?"

Adam and Eve were ashamed of themselves. God banished them from the Garden of Eden and said to Adam, "You have to slave for food." He turned to Eve and said, "You shall bear children, but it will be painful." Then He turned to the serpent and said, "You shall crawl on your belly for the rest of your life."

08 Adam's Despair

God made clothes out of animal skin for Adam and Eve before He sent them out of the Garden of Eden. To the east side of the garden, God sent a mighty winged angel to guard its entrance. A flaming sword that turned in all directions protected the way to the Tree of Knowledge and Life.

Adam and Eve were ashamed but they had to face the consequences of what they had done. As they were leaving the Garden of Eden, God said to them, "Because of what you have done, now thorns will grow amongst the crops, the daily life will become more difficult and one day you both will die. I made you from dust and one day you will return to dust."

09 Cain and Abel

Adam and Eve had two sons, Cain and Abel. Cain was a farmer while Abel was a shepherd. One day, Cain offered his crops to God while Abel brought a lamb as a sacrifice. God could see into both their hearts. He knew that Abel really wanted to please Him, whereas he could see the jealous nature of Cain.

So God looked favourably upon Abel's offering which made Cain jealous. One day, they were both out in a field and Cain killed Abel. When God asked him where Abel was, Cain said he didn't know. God knew what had happened and said, "The ground which is stained with your brother's blood would no longer grow crop. You would have to spend your life as a wanderer." Cain felt his punishment was harsh and also that his life would be in danger, if anyone knew what he had done. So God put a mark upon his forehead that no one would kill Cain.

10 The Story of the Flood

Abel's murder was the beginning of violence and wickedness in the world. Soon people started displeasing God. He was very sad to see His beautiful world like this. He felt sorry for creating Man. He decided to cleanse His Earth of all the wicked people. But in all this evil, there was one good man, Noah, who pleased God in all his ways.

So God wanted to save Noah, his wife, their three sons, Ham, Shem and Japheth.

"I am going to cleanse the world," God told Noah.

"Build for yourself a special boat; a mighty ark. Make it out of timber and put rooms in it. Build it with three decks; make only one window and one door."

11 Noah's Ark

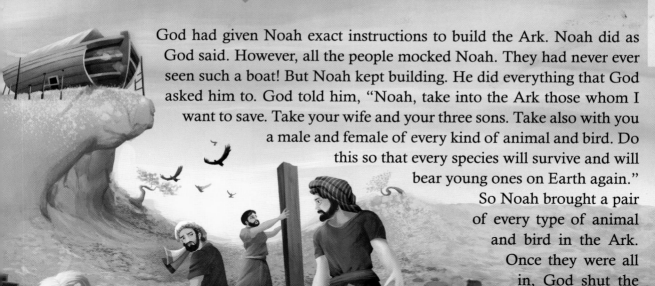

God had given Noah exact instructions to build the Ark. Noah did as God said. However, all the people mocked Noah. They had never ever seen such a boat! But Noah kept building. He did everything that God asked him to. God told him, "Noah, take into the Ark those whom I want to save. Take your wife and your three sons. Take also with you a male and female of every kind of animal and bird. Do this so that every species will survive and will bear young ones on Earth again."

So Noah brought a pair of every type of animal and bird in the Ark. Once they were all in, God shut the door of the Ark.

12 The Great Flood

Noah, his family and all the creatures he had chosen were in the Ark along with food supplies. Then seven days later, the flood came. Rain fell from the sky in torrents and it did not stop for forty days. The flood rose up from the ground. The Ark began to float. The water kept on rising.

Soon it covered the mountains, and still it went on rising. Every creature that lived on the Earth died. The water remained for 150 days!

Only those who were sheltered with Noah in the Ark were safe. Noah thanked God for his help and promised to always love Him and the things He had created.

13 The Flood Recedes

God had not forgotten Noah and the animals in the Ark. After many days had passed, He stopped the rain. The storm clouds blew away and the water no longer welled up. Slowly and gradually, the floodwaters started ebbing away. Then, in a few days, the Ark came to rest on a mountaintop in the Ararat range.

The waters went down further, till at last, one could see the tops of the mountains, clearly. Forty days later, Noah opened a window and sent out a raven. The raven did not return, but flew over the Earth till the waters had gone down. After some time, Noah sent out a dove. It could not find anywhere to land, so it flew back to the Ark. Noah understood that the land was still not visible and they will have to remain in the Ark for a few more days.

14 The Promise of a Rainbow

After a few days, God told Noah to leave the Ark. Noah and his family rejoiced hearing the news and rushed out of the Ark on to the land.

At once, Noah built an altar and offered a sacrifice of the animals. God was pleased and He blessed Noah. God put a beautiful rainbow in the sky, promising Noah that He would never again do something like this to the Earth. There will always be seeds and harvest, cold and heat, winter and summer, day and night.

The rainbow is a reminder that God has never broken His promise and He never will.

15 The Tower of Babel

All the people of the world came from Noah and his off springs. Thus, everybody on Earth spoke the same language. One group of wandering people decided to settle in the land of Babylonia and built a beautiful city. They also decided to make a very, tall tower that reached into heaven. The thing was, they could all agree, because in the time after the flood, everyone spoke the same language.

They all could work together. So God began to confuse the language of the people on Earth. People started calling things by different names. Soon the people weren't getting along anymore. They decided to quit building the great city and the tower. So the magnificent tower never got finished. It became known as the tower of Babel because that's where God made all the people's language sound like babbling to each other.

16 Abraham and the Covenant

Abraham was a descendent of Shem who was the son of Noah. One day, God told Abraham to leave his home in Ur and move to a land in Canaan.

God said, "I promise that I will bless you, and make your family great. I will be with you in all you do, and because of you all the families of the Earth will be blessed."

Abraham obeyed God. He took Sarah his wife, and Lot, his nephew, along with his cattle and servants and reached Canaan.

But Abraham was sad for he had no children. Yet, Abraham never doubted God's promise to him. He always obeyed God without questioning or doubting Him.

17 Lot Chooses First

Abraham and Lot both had a large flock of sheep and herds of cattle. So it was very difficult to find enough pasture and water for both. To avoid enmity, Abraham advised Lot to choose a part of the land and live separately. Although Abraham was older, he allowed Lot to choose first.

Lot chose the plains of Jordan, near the cities of Sodom and Gomorrah, and settled there. They were well watered and fertile.

Abraham remained in Canaan. The Lord spoke to Abraham, "Look at the land from where you are standing. Look to the north, south, east and west. I will give all this land that you see, to you and your descendants."

18 Angelic Visitors for Abraham

One day, three men came to meet Abraham. He welcomed them and washed their dusty feet and after seating them under a tree, served them food and milk.

As the visitors were pleased with Abraham's hospitality, they blessed Abraham saying that Sarah would have a baby. Sarah and Abraham were quite old, so Sarah gently laughed to herself.

The visitor asked Abraham, "Why did Sarah laugh? Is anything too difficult for the Lord?"

It was then that Abraham realised that the stranger spoke with the voice of God.

19 At Lot's House

The people of Sodom and Gomorrah led a sinful life. So God decided to destroy the cities and told Abraham about it. Abraham remembered that his nephew Lot resided in Sodom and begged God to spare the cities.

God told him that he would spare the city if there were ten good people living there. That evening God sent two angels to visit Lot's house.

Suddenly, a mob gathered around Lot's house and demanded to hand over the guests to them, so that they could torture them. Lot begged the mob to go away and spare the guests, but the mob grew angrier and proceeded to attack Lot. The angels pulled Lot inside and shut the door. God saw the chaos and decided to spare Lot and his family, but destroyed both the cities.

20 Sodom and Gomorrah

God had decided to destroy the cities of Sodom and Gomorrah because of their sinful lifestyle. Abraham's nephew, Lot, was a good man and lived his life following the God's words faithfully. So God declared that only Lot, his wife and two daughters were the only good people living there. So, He sent two Angels to take them out of the city. God asked Lot and his family not to look back. Then, God poured fire and sulphur from Heaven, completely destroying Sodom and Gomorrah. As Lot and his family were fleeing the city, Lot's wife gave in to her curiosity and turned back. Just as she looked at the city, she became a pillar of salt because she disobeyed God. Only Lot and his two daughters escaped without getting hurt.

21 The Birth of Isaac

The Lord did as He had promised Abraham many years ago.

When Abraham was 100 years old and Sarah was 90 years, Sarah was blessed with a child! Abraham named his son Isaac, meaning 'He Laughs', because Sarah laughed when she came to know that she was going to have a son.

On the eighth day, after his son was born, Abraham circumcised Isaac, as God had commanded him to do.

God had honoured Abraham's faith.

22 Isaac and Ishmael

When Sarah had lost hope of conceiving a child, she allowed her handmaiden Hagar to become Abraham's wife. Hagar was blessed with a boy, Ishmael. But after Isaac's birth, Sarah grew jealous of Ishmael.

One day Sarah saw Ishmael making fun of Isaac and she was furious. She told Abraham, "You have to get rid of that hand maiden and her son."

Abraham was reluctant to obey his wife as Ishmael was his own son as well. God came to his rescue and said, "Listen to Sarah and let Ishmael and Hagar go. I will look after them." The next day, Abraham gave some food and a water container made of goat skin to Hagar and Ishmael, and bid them farewell.

23 Ishmael and Hagar

Ishmael and Hagar left Abraham and wandered in the desert of Beersheba. Hagar knew that surviving in the barren desert will become very difficult, once their food and water finished. Just then an exhausted Ishmael started crying. Hagar laid him in the shade of a bush and started sobbing, as she realised that she may lose her son.

God heard Ishmael cry and spoke to Hagar, "Do not fear, for I will take care of your son and his descendants."

Saying so, He guided Hagar to a well of pure water. Hagar took water and rushed to her son. As Ishmael drank the water, Hagar knew that God will look over him.

Ishmael grew up to be a strong man. It is widely believed that he is the ancestor of Arab people.

24 Abraham and Isaac

One day, God told Abraham to take young Isaac to Mount Moriah and offer him as a sacrifice. Without any protest, Abraham set out with two servants, a donkey, some wood and Isaac to Mount Moriah. When they reached the mountain, only Abraham and Isaac climbed it.

Then, Abraham built an altar, placed the wood, tied Isaac and laid him on it. As Abraham raised the knife to kill Isaac, the Angel of the Lord spoke, "Stop! God knows that you love him because you were ready to sacrifice your son to him."

Overjoyed, Abraham caught a ram and offered wit as a sacrifice. For the faith that Abraham had showed in God, He blessed Abraham and Isaac.

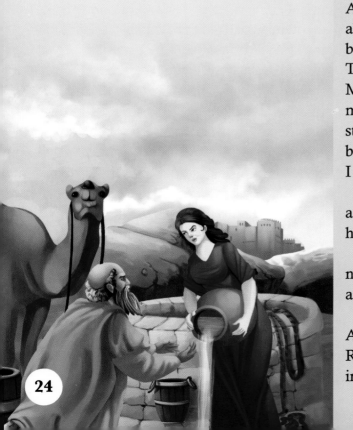

25 Isaac and Rebekah

After Sarah's death, Abraham was worried about Isaac. Abraham told his servant to bring back a bride for Isaac from Mesopotamia. The servant travelled to the city of Nahor, Mesopotamia. He prayed to God, "Please let me meet the one you have chosen for Isaac. I will stand beside that well and wait for a girl to come by. I shall ask for a drink and if she offers water, I will recognise the one you have chosen."

Soon, a girl came to the well. The servant asked for some water. The girl smiled and gave him water.

The servant asked the girl her name, "My name is Rebekah, I am the daughter of Bethuel and granddaughter of Nahor."

The servant realised that Nahor was Abraham's brother's name. He went home with Rebekah. The servant asked for Rebekah's hand in marriage for Isaac and the family agreed.

26 Isaac and his Sons

Isaac and Rebekah were happily married, but even after years they didn't have any child. Isaac prayed to God and He told Isaac, "Your second-born child will be stronger than the first born."

Soon Rebekah gave birth to twin sons, Esau and Jacob. Both brothers were very different from each other. Esau loved outdoor and became a skilled huntsman. But Jacob loved to work indoors. Esau was Isaac's favourite.

One day, Esau came back from hunting, while Jacob was cooking. Esau said, "Give me some soup, brother. I am dying of hunger." Jacob said, "I will give you soup only if you give me your birthright as the first born." Without thinking, Esau replied, "Alright, I give you my birthright as the firstborn." Jacob gave some soup and bread to Esau. Esau happily gulped it all down and left to hunt again.

27 Isaac Blesses Jacob

When Isaac grew old, he lost his eyesight. He realised that he didn't have much long to live and it was time to give his first born, Esau, his blessings. He called Esau and told him to kill a deer, cook a stew and give it to him. Esau left immediately to hunt. Jacob overheard the conversation and told Rebekah. She decided to cheat Isaac.

She made goat stew and asked Jacob to give it to his father. Jacob did exactly what his mother said and gave Isaac the goat stew. Isaac asked his son, "How did you manage to kill a deer and cook a stew so fast?" Jacob replied, "Because God guided me." Isaac gave Jacob his blessing. When Esau realised that Jacob has taken his birthright and blessings, he vows to kill Jacob. Rebekah fearing for her son's life asked Jacob to run away to Mesopotamia and save his life.

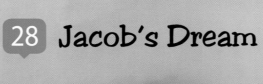

28 Jacob's Dream

As per Rebekah's instructions, Jacob fled to Mesopotamia, his mother's land and hid from his brother, Esau. On the first day of his journey, which would take many days to complete, he decided to take some rest as the sun was going down. As soon as he fell asleep, he had a dream.

He saw a staircase stretched out to the heavens from earth and angels were ascending the stairs. Then, God said, "I give you this land on which you are lying down. I will bless you and your descendants, and will take care of them wherever they go." Jacob woke up and thought, "I was not aware that God resides in this place."

The next morning, he placed the stone he was lying on as a pillar and poured oil over it to anoint it. He named the place Bethel, which means 'the house of God'.

29 Jacob and the Trickster

When Jacob reached Haran, Mesopotamia, he saw a young girl in the field and asked her, "Do you know my Uncle Laban?" The girl replied, "My name is Rachel and I am the daughter of Laban. Come, I shall take you to him."

Laban was very pleased to see his nephew and agreed to let Jacob rear his sheep for him. Jacob said, "I shall work for seven years, but after that you have to allow me to marry your daughter Rachel."

Laban agreed to Jacob's terms. After seven years, he kept his promise but instead of making Rachel the bride, he married Leah his elder daughter to Jacob. Jacob was furious, but Laban reminded him that according to the tradition, Jacob can have several wives. Rachel became Jacob's second wife. Jacob had four wives, out of which three wives (except Rachel) gave birth to sons. Later God blessed Rachel with one son, Joseph.

30 Jacob and Esau

Jacob lived happily with his wives and sons in Haran for several years. One night, God came in Jacob's dream and told him to go back to Canaan. The very next day, Jacob with his wives and children set out for Canaan. When they reached near Canaan, he set up tents and sent messengers to Esau with gifts.

One night, a stranger grabbed Jacob. The man touched Jacob's hips and put it out of joint. The stranger asked Jacob's name and said, "From now on, you shall be called Israel," which meant 'he struggles with God', saying so, the stranger disappeared.

The next morning, Jacob heard that his brother Esau was coming to meet him and became very nervous. But when Esau met Jacob, he took Jacob in his arms and embraced him lovingly. Esau accepted the gifts from Jacob and finished any animosity between them.

31 The Story of Joseph

Rachel, Jacob's second wife, gave birth to her second son, Benjamin, but she died soon after that. Jacob was distraught after Rachel's death, as he loved her the most. Joseph became his favourite son, a fact which did not go unnoticed by his other sons and became a great source of jealousy for them.

Jacob gifted Joseph a multi-coloured robe, which made his brothers grow angrier with him. Even though surrounded by his half-siblings, Joseph loved them a lot and always shared his strange dreams with them. But the messages from dream did not please the brothers as he Joseph always seemed superior to them in his dreams. His brothers called him a 'dreamer'.

01 Joseph's Dreams

Joseph was Jacob's eleventh and favourite son. Unlike his half-brothers, Joseph was a dreamer and he always insisted on sharing his dreams with his brothers, no matter how much it annoyed them. One day, Joseph told them, "Last night I saw a dream where we all were in the fields and tying up sheaves of corn. Suddenly, the sheaf that I was tying stood up. After that, all your sheaves also stood up, made a circle around my sheaf and bowed down to it. Isn't it amazing?"

The brothers were very annoyed to hear the dream and one of them asked, "Do you want to say that we should make a circle around you and bow down to you?" Joseph's half-brothers were aware of their father's partiality to him, which was a great source of jealousy and hatred for Joseph to them.

02 Joseph's Dreams were Messages

Out of twelve sons of Jacob, Joseph was a dreamer. He was as hard-working as his brothers, but always had strange dreams which he used to share with his family. One day, Joseph sat down with his father and brothers and shared the dream he had.

He said, "Last night I saw a very strange dream. In it, the sun, the moon and the eleven stars bowed down to me." The brothers did not say anything, but the remark of "eleven stars" did not go unnoticed to them. Jacob, however, was very annoyed by the dream and asked, "Does that mean that you want your parents and your brothers to bow down to you too?" But Joseph's dream made Jacob think that maybe Joseph had a higher purpose to serve on Earth.

03 Joseph in the Well

One day, Joseph's eleven brothers were away from the house, taking care of the flock of sheep. Jacob called Joseph and said, "Your brothers have taken the sheep to the field. Take their food with you and see if everything is alright."

After reaching the field he could not see his brothers. He enquired from a man about his brothers, who told him that his brothers had gone to Dothan, a nearby village. In the fields near Dothan, one of the brothers spied that Joseph was coming their way and they hid behind a huge boulder. He said, "Let's kill him now."

Rueben, Jacob's eldest son, said, "No, we will not kill our brother. We will throw him in a well to teach him a lesson." As soon as Joseph came near the boulder, the brothers caught him, stripped his robe away and threw him the well.

04 Joseph is Sold

Rueben, Jacob's eldest son, went away with his flock of sheep after he pushed Joseph in the well and the other brothers sat down to eat their lunch. Soon, they saw a group of merchants approaching the fields. The merchants told them that they were carrying spices to Egypt.

Judah, Jacob's second son, said, "Let's sell Joseph to them. He is anyway quite useless to us." The other brothers agreed and sold Joseph to the merchants for twenty pieces of silver. When Rueben came back, he was shocked to hear from his brothers that they had sold Joseph. They decided that they could not tell their father this, so they killed a goat, smeared Joseph's robe with its blood and took it to their father. Jacob saw Joseph's robe and said, "I will die mourning the death of my son, Joseph."

05 Joseph, the Slave

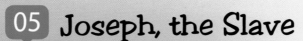

The merchants who had bought Joseph reached Egypt and sold him to the captain of the Pharaoh's guards. Joseph worked very hard in the house, which was noticed by Potiphar, the captain. He made Joseph in charge of the whole household. But Potiphar's wife was entranced by Joseph's good looks. She tried her best to entice him, but was rejected by Joseph. He said, "My master, your husband, has been very kind to me. I cannot cheat him like this."

She cornered him one day in her room, but he ran away. She screamed for help and told everyone that Joseph tried to take advantage of her. Potiphar believed his wife and finally put him in jail. Joseph didn't lose hope and continued to work hard in the jail as well.

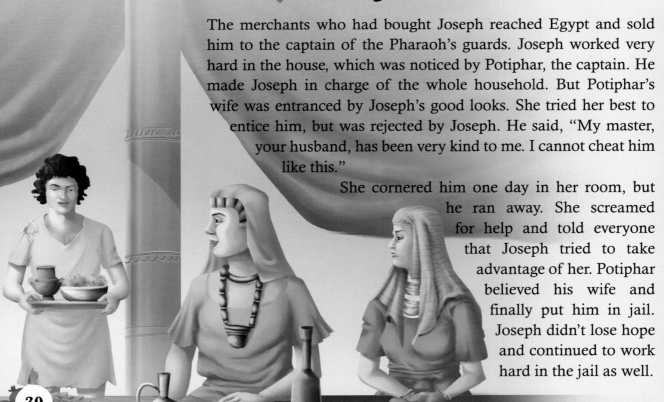

06 Joseph in Prison

One day, the Pharaoh's butler and baker were put in jail. Joseph, who was touted as a hard-working inmate in the jail, was put in charge of overlooking their work. Both the inmates had strange dreams, which they told Joseph.

The butler said, "I saw a grapevine with three branches. I plucked out a grape and squeezed wine into Pharaoh's cup. What does it mean?"

Joseph replied, "It means that in three days time, you will be released from jail and will go back to work for the Pharaoh. When the dream comes true, please do me a favour and mention me to the Pharaoh." The butler was very pleased and promised to mention Joseph's name to the Pharaoh once he was free.

07 The Baker's Dream

While in prison, Pharaoh's baker and butler had strange dreams. They asked Joseph to interpret the dreams for them. After Joseph interpreted the butler's dream, the baker told Joseph about his dream. He said, "In my dream, I was carrying three baskets on my head. The top basket had breads, but the birds kept coming and pecking on it. It was a strange dream, but what does it mean?"

Joseph replied, "In three days time, the Pharaoh will sentence you to death." The baker was very unhappy to hear about it. After three days, the butler's and the baker's dreams came true. Pharaoh wanted to throw a party and called the butler back to join his post, but gave a death sentence to the baker.

08 The Pharaoh's Dreams

The Pharaoh's butler, after being freed, had forgotten all about his promise to Joseph. He lived a content life, serving the Pharaoh for two years. One night, the Pharaoh had a strange dream. He woke up feeling very restless. He immediately called his minister and asked them to search for the most learned men and magicians who would be able to interpret his strange dream. But none of them could do it, leaving the Pharaoh feeling more restless than before.

Then, the butler remembered Joseph and his promise to him. He told the Pharaoh about Joseph and how he had interpreted his dream correctly.

09 Joseph and the Pharaoh

Joseph was pleased to be summoned by the Pharaoh to interpret his strange dreams. The Pharaoh said, "I had two strange dreams. In the first dream I saw seven healthy cows come out of the River Nile, followed by seven famished cows. The famished cows devoured the healthy cows. In the second dream, I saw seven ripe ears of wheat grow on a single stalk and seven thin ears of wheat on another single stalk. The thin ears then ate up the ripe ears."

Joseph replied, "Both dreams mean the same thing. Egypt will see seven years of good harvest, followed by seven years of famine. You must make sure that you save grain for the famine, so that people don't suffer during it." The Pharaoh was impressed by Joseph and made him a minister responsible for storing grains for the famine. Joseph did his work diligently and saved up enough grains for the famine. As he had predicted, Egypt had good harvest for seven years followed by seven years of bad harvest.

10 Joseph's Brothers

Joseph travelled all over Egypt and set up various stores of grains in the cities. In the seven years of good harvest, he stored enough grains for the whole of Egypt and more. As the famine hit Egypt, people went to the Pharaoh to ask for help. The Pharaoh directed them to Joseph, who started selling the stored grains to the people. He had stored up so much grain that he started selling the grain to nearby countries affected by famine.

In Canaan, Joseph's brothers and their families were suffering from starvation. They heard that Egypt was selling grains. One of the brothers said, "I have heard that the Pharaoh had appointed a very responsible minister to store grains during their good harvest time. We must approach him, lest we die of hunger." When the brothers told Jacob about their plans, he said, "You must go and appeal to the minister in Egypt. As Benjamin is very young, he shall stay back with me." The ten brothers set out for a gruelling journey through tough terrains. When they reached Egypt, they were weak and their clothes were torn.

11 Joseph Meets his Brothers

When Joseph saw his ten brothers from Canaan in Egypt, he remembered how they sold him off as a slave. The brothers approached him, without realising that he was their brother. Joseph pretended that he didn't. One of the brothers said, "We have come here to buy grains." Joseph cried out, "You are lying. You all are spies!"

The brothers said, "We are not spies. We were twelve brothers, one died and the other one is at home with our father." When Joseph heard about Benjamin, he craved to see his younger brother. He said, "Prove your innocence to me. Bring back your youngest brother to me. Meanwhile, one of you will remain here as my prisoner." The brothers went back to Canaan, leaving Simeon behind as Joseph's prisoner. Joseph instructed the men packing the grain for his brother to slip money inside the sacks.

12 The Brothers Return to Bring Benjamin

The nine sons of Jacob returned to Canaan with grains from Egypt. Jacob was very happy to see them and asked them, "How was the journey? Were you successful in your endeavour?" The brothers were very unhappy, as they thought that the bad days they had to face was a consequence of what they did to Joseph. One of them told Jacob, "We have got the grain but the minister of Egypt accused of being spies and told us that we have to take Benjamin to prove our innocence. He has imprisoned Simeon."

Jacob was sad to hear about Simeon, but refused to let his sons take Benjamin to Egypt. When they opened the sacks, the brother found the money with grains. After the family had eaten the grains, Jacob asked his sons to go back to Egypt to buy more grain. His sons persuaded him to let Benjamin come along and free Simeon from prison and Jacob reluctantly agreed.

13 The Silver Cup

Jacob sent spices and nuts as gifts for the minister. When the brothers reached the minister's house in Egypt, Joseph was overwhelmed to see his younger brother. He asked his men to release Simeon from jail and allowed him to join his brothers for the feast at his place. The brothers were surprised with such a gesture and enjoyed the feast at Joseph's home. Meanwhile, Joseph ordered their sacks to be filled with grains and the money given by the brothers to be kept back in the sack. He also asked the men to keep a silver cup in Benjamin's sack.

The next morning, when the brothers started their journey to Canaan, the minister's men stopped them and accused them of stealing their master's silver cup. They checked all the sacks and found the cup in Benjamin's sack and arrested him.

14 Joseph Reunites with Brothers

When Benjamin was arrested for stealing a silver cup from Joseph's house, Joseph announced that he would keep Benjamin as his servant. Judah stepped forward and said that he refused to let his brother stay, as it would break their father's heart. Joseph sent his servants away. He spoke to his brothers in their native language. He said, "I am Joseph, your brother. Whatever happened in the past let it be in the past. I believe God had sent me here to help my family during the famine. As we have five more years of famine yet to come, I would like you all to shift here, with me, in Egypt."

He sent his brothers back to Canaan, to fetch Jacob and the rest of the family to Egypt with gifts for Jacob, with permission from the Pharaoh. Jacob was overjoyed to hear that Joseph was alive and he moved to settle down in the area of Goshen, in Egypt. Joseph took care of his family, and made sure they were well provided with supplies.

15 The History of Egypt

The land of Egypt was a prosperous land in the time of the Old Testament. The River Nile was a very important river, and the major agricultural land was around the river. Many wanderers came and settled in Egypt, among which the Israelites (descendants of Jacob) were the majority. Gradually, they became very rich and held very important positions in Egypt.

The Egyptians worshipped around 2000 gods and goddesses and the Pharaoh was considered a god himself. The pharaoh was also the head of the government, society and religion. The Egyptians had knowledge about medicine, maths, writing and architecture. They built many temples and pyramids for their gods and pharaohs. After the death of Joseph, a new pharaoh came into power, Ramases II. The Pharaoh had a dislike for the Israelites and was alarmed to see their population increase in Egypt and gain power.

16 The Israelites in Egypt

Isaac's people, the Israelites, under his son Jacob's guidance, moved to Egypt and settled there. The Pharaoh was afraid that the Israelites were prospering, multiplying and becoming very strong. Soon the Pharaoh told his subjects, "We have too many foreigners dwelling among us. They might turn on us and take control of our land. We must find a way to stop them from becoming too powerful."

The Pharaoh soon declared that all Israelites would be enslaved. The Egyptians tried to crush their spirits by making them work hard on construction sites. They were pressed into slavery. But the more the Egyptians oppressed the Israelites, the more they grew in number.

17 Baby Moses

To tackle the increasing population of Israelites, the Pharaoh ordered all the Israelite male babies to be thrown into the Nile. The soldiers entered the Israelite's dwelling to carry out the King's order and ruthlessly snatched the newborn boys and threw them in the Nile.

Jochebed, an Israelite woman, was scared for her baby boy. She hid him for months, but realised that she won't be able to do so for long.

She made a reed basket and floated it down the river, putting her daughter Miriam, on watch. The basket flowed in the river and into the Pharaoh's palace.

Pharaoh's daughter, who came there with her maidens to bathe, noticed the basket. One of her maids brought it to her. Seeing the poor little baby crying, she decided to keep him as her son! She called him Moses meaning 'drawn out of water'!

Jochebed was called by her to nurse Moses and he grew up in Pharaoh's palace as a prince.

18 Prince in Egypt

Moses grew up in Pharaoh's palace as a Prince of Egypt. He learnt all the skills of the Egyptians like reading, writing and fighting.

But as a child, his nurse Jochebed confided to him about his true lineage. While growing up, he never forgot that he was an Israelite and that the slaves in Pharaoh's palace were really his own people. He witnessed the mistreatment of his people by the Egyptians and yearned to do something about it.

19 Moses and his People

One day, Moses saw an Egyptian slave driver beating a Israelite slave. Unable to control his anger, he pushed the slave driver. The slave driver, caught by surprise, fell down and hit his head against a stone and bled to death.

He knew that the punishment for killing any Egyptian is death and so, horrified at what he had done, he ran away.

The next day when Moses saw two Israelites fighting, he tried to stop them. But they fearfully asked him if he would kill them too! Moses immediately understood that everybody knew about the crime he committed. So, he fled from Egypt.

20 Moses and the Burning Bush

After fleeing from Egypt, Moses reached Midian and rescued Priest Jethro's seven daughters from some shepherds who were troubling them. Later, Jethro thanked him and gave him shelter. Moses married Zipporah, Jethro's daughter, and became a shepherd.

One day, on his way back from the desert of Horeb, the mountain of God, he saw a bush on fire, but it was not burning up. Then God spoke to him. He explained that Moses was the leader, chosen to save the Israelites from Pharaoh's cruelty. He assured him that he will guide and help Moses in the chosen path. God told Moses to throw down his staff and gave it back to him saying, "Behold the staff. With this staff, you shall do many wonders."

21 Moses Goes to Pharaoh

Moses asked his father-in-law's permission to leave the animals and travel back to Egypt, with his family. On the way, he met Aaron, his brother. Moses told his brother about his mission to free his people. Together they confronted the Pharaoh, at his palace. Moses said, "Pharaoh of Egypt, free my people."

Pharaoh mocked, "You can't expect me to let my slaves go. In fact, I think the Israelites should work harder!"

The Pharaoh got so angry that he ordered the slave drivers, "The Israelites had been given straw to strengthen the mud bricks they made. Now they had to find their own straw and still make as many bricks."

22 Moses Meets Pharaoh Again

God spoke to Moses, "You must tell the Pharaoh to let my people go. If he doesn't, then I will have to unleash the ten plagues over his kingdom."

Reluctantly, the two men returned to Pharaoh with their request. When the Pharaoh was not convinced, after Moses repeatedly asked him to free the Israelites, God decided to unleash the ten plagues on Egypt.

First, the river Nile turned into blood! All the fish died. Next, God sent frogs all over the land. Then, God turned the dust into lice, crawling on man and beast. After this, swarms of flies flew everywhere. Then, the cattle became ill and died; hail destroyed the crops; an epidemic of skin disease that caused sores and boils; and locusts destroyed and ate everything. But the Pharaoh still would not let the people go.

23 The Plagues of Egypt

Disease struck the cattle. An epidemic of a skin disease broke out that caused open sores and painful boils but the Pharaoh remained unmoved at the suffering of his own people. Moses warned him of another disaster: a storm of hail that would destroy all the crops.

In the midst of the storm, the Pharaoh admitted he was wrong, and begged Moses to pray to his God for the hail to stop. When all was calm, he changed his mind but the locusts destroyed the crops that escaped the hail. Again, the Pharaoh begged Moses to pray to his God for the locusts to stop and later again he changed his mind.

Then, God sent three days of absolute darkness over Egypt. The last and tenth plague was most terrible. All the Egyptian firstborn, of both man and cattle, including Pharaoh's son, died as the Angel of Death passed over at midnight.

24 The Passover

When God commanded the tenth and last plague upon Egypt, He instructed Moses what the Israelites needed to do. God said, "On the 10th day of the month, every Israelite family will take a young sheep and kill it on the 14th day. Then paint the blood of the sheep around the entrance of their house using hyssop leaves as a brush. The Angel of Death would spare only these homes when he passed over at midnight."

Moses explained God's instructions to the people. The faithful people did as they were told. Exactly as God said, the Angel of Death passed over Egypt at midnight and spared the blood-marked houses. The first born in every home without the blood mark upon it, died.

25 The Israelites are Released

After the last plague was unleashed by God. A terrible cry rose all over Egypt. Finally, Pharaoh let the Israelites leave, ending 430 years of bitter slavery and so Moses finally led his people out of Egypt.

It was the start of a journey to the land of Canaan, the place which God had promised Abraham. Moses said to the people, "Remember this day—the day on which you left Egypt, the place where you were slaves. The Lord has solemnly promised to give you the land of Canaan. When he brings you into that rich and fertile land, you must celebrate the Passover festival in the first month of every year. You shall tell the story of the celebration to your children, to remember what God did for you today."

26 Pharaoh's Anger

God told Moses to lead the Israelites through the desert. God's cloudy pillar led them by day while a pillar of fire gave them light by night.

"See!" the people said, "The Lord is leading us."

However, back in Egypt, when the Pharaoh heard about the slaves, he grew angry. Refusing to accept defeat, he took his chariot along with 600 other captains to bring them back!

"Quick! Assemble the army and its finest soldiers. We shall not let the slaves go away," he ordered.

Pharaoh and his army reached the place near the Red Sea, where the Israelites had set up their camps. When they saw the Pharaoh's army coming closer. The people got scared and turned to Moses.

27 Crossing the Red Sea

The Israelites had no way to escape the Pharaoh's army and so they began to blame Moses. "Your so-called bid for freedom has failed. Now, we will die here in the desert. It would have been better if we had stayed in Egypt as slaves."

"Do not fear!" Moses calmed them, "I have often felt discouraged myself. But have faith, God will help us and defend us. Stand still and see the salvation of God. He will fight for you."

Then God spoke to Moses and told him to raise his staff and hold it out over the Red Sea. A strong wind started to blow and Moses struck down his staff in the water. The Red Sea simply parted and walls of water stood on both sides. While the Israelites were crossing, God troubled the Pharaoh with the fiery pillar and delayed the army from attacking the Israelites.

28 Rejoice the Lord

The Egyptians were afraid, yet they followed the Israelites. After all, the Israelites had crossed over, the Egyptians were in the middle of the Red Sea. The Egyptian army looked in alarm at the water on either side.

Just then, God told Moses to hold his hand over the sea. As soon as Moses held his hand over the Red Sea, the sea closed up. It rolled in over the pathway where the Egyptian army stood. They all shouted and cried but soon, the entire Egyptian army drowned.

Moses and his people looked at the wonder that had just happened. They were all amazed at the power of the God who had saved them. They all began to celebrate their escape. Then Moses and his people sang praises to God for He had freed from centuries of bitter slavery.

01 Wanderings in the Wilderness

The Israelites were kept under slavery in Egypt for centuries, till Moses came and gave them freedom. After barely escaping the Egyptian army and crossing the Red Sea, Moses led the Israelites to Canaan through Sinai, to avoid the usual Egyptian trade routes. But the land of Sinai was hot and barren, with no respite in sight.

The people grew restless and thirsty with each passing day and complained to Moses. Moses encouraged them to keep moving, telling them that God will look out for them. One day, the Israelites reached a small oasis, but found out that the water was foul and bitter. Then, God spoke to Moses and asked him to throw the stick near his feet into the oasis. As soon as Moses obeyed God's words, the water in the oasis turned fresh and sweet. The Israelites were able to revive themselves and move to a bigger oasis ahead. There, they pitched their tents and settles down for few days.

02 Food from the Sky

Moses told the Israelites that they will have to keep moving towards Canaan, after resting near an oasis for a few days. The Israelites gathered their belongings and continued their journey to Canaan. For many days they did not come across any oasis and people grew restless and tired.

They complained to Moses that maybe they were happy being slaves in Egypt, rather than following Moses and dying in the desert. God heard people's complaint and spoke to Moses. He said, "I shall help only if they agree to obey me. Tell my people that tomorrow they will get to eat meat. From the next day onwards, I shall provide food to help them to survive. They may collect as much food they want for six days, but on the seventh day they will have to take rest." Moses told the people about God's command. The next day, quails flew down to the people, which they caught and cooked. Thus, God kept his promise to people and the Israelites were happy.

03 Special Food in the Desert

God sent down quails to the Israelites to eat, as they made their journey through a desert to Canaan. The next morning, Israelites woke up to find the ground covered with dew. As the sun came up, the dew got dried up to form a white, flaky stuff. Israelites picked it up and ate it, and were surprised to find that the flakes were delicious and sweet. The white, flaky food was called 'manna' which mean 'what-is-it'. God provided manna for six days and the Israelites collected as much as they could to last them for many days. On the sixth day, Moses reminded Israelites that the next day is the day of Sabbath, which means the day they have to take rest and should not go out to collect food. On the day of Sabbath, some disobeyed God and went out looking for food, but could not find any.

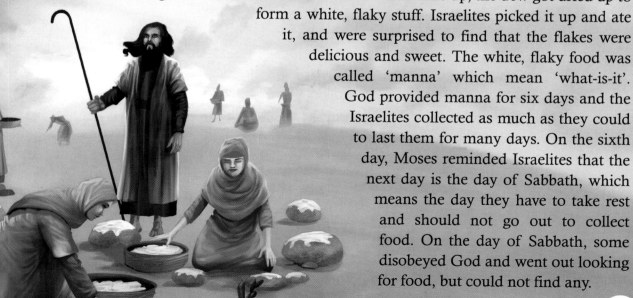

04 Water in the Wilderness

As the Israelites continued on their journey through the desert to reach Canaan they reached a settlement called Rephidim but didn't find any water. They grew thirsty and complained to Moses and blamed him. Moses became angry and asked, "Why do you all blame me for your woes? When you complaint to me, you complaint about God. Has He not helped to escape you slavery and provided you food when you needed it?"

But Israelites were adamant and continued to complaint to Moses. Then God said to him, "Go to a small hill nearby and I will guide you." Moses took some elder Israelites with him, away from the settlement and saw a small rocky hill. He climbed it, raised his staff to God and struck it down. A small stream of water erupted from the place. The elders drank the water and found it fresh and sweet. Israelites realised that God indeed kept His promises.

05 Moses Wins the Amalekites

The Amalekites were a wandering tribe in the land of Sinai, who refused to share their oasis with other wanderers. When they saw the Israelites settle down in Rephisim, they attacked them. Moses asked a young man, Joshua, to gather the strongest men among the Israelites to fight the Amalekites.

The next morning, Moses went up a nearby hill with his brother Aaron and another man name Hur. He stood there with his staff raised above his head. The Amalekites watched Moses from a distance and waited till he takes his arms down. When Moses got tired, he put his arms down and the Amalekites attacked. But the Israelites were ready and fought bravely. Moses raised his hands again and it gave courage to the Israelites to fight bravely. When Moses's arms got tired, Aaron and Hur stood beside him and each held up one of his arms to keep the Israelites motivated. By sun down, the Amalekites were driven away and Moses thanked God by building an altar on the hill overlooking Rephidim.

06 Sharing the Work

One day, Jethro visited Moses in the desert, along with Moses's wife, Zipporah and their two sons, Gershom and Eliezer. Jethro was very proud of Moses and with his faith in God.

The next day, Jethro noticed long lines of people waiting outside Moses's tent. Moses explained that he solved problems brought by the people; he would teach them God's laws and pray to God on their behalf.

Jethro was disturbed and said, "There are too many for you to manage alone. The people will wear you out. Delegate the responsibilities to the heads of the tribes. If there is anything they can't handle, the people can approach you." Moses liked the idea and delegated the responsibility to solve problems and teach the law to the heads of the tribe.

07 God Speaks to Moses

After travelling for three months, the Israelites camped at the foot of Mount Sinai in the wilderness. God called out from the mountain and Moses climbed Mount Sinai to speak with Him. "Here is my message for the Israelites," God said, "say to them, that I have brought you safely out of Egypt, as an eagle carries young on its wings. If they obey me and live in agreement with me, then they will be my special people." Moses told them what God had said and he also told them to prepare to worship God from the foot of the mountain. God called Moses to Mount Senai again and told him that He will give Moses the instructions, which every Israelite will have to follow.

08 Mount Sinai

God told Moses at the Mount Senai, "I am the Lord, your God, the one who brought you out of Egypt where you were slaves. Worship no god but me. Do not make for yourselves images of anything in Heaven or on Earth or in the water under the Earth. Do not bow down to any idol or worship it because I am the Lord, your God. I bring punishment on those who hate me and on their descendants down to the third and fourth generation. But I show my love to thousands of generations of those who love me and obey my laws. Do not use my name for evil purposes, for I will punish anyone who misuses my name. Observe the Sabbath and keep it holy. You have six days in which to do your work, but the seventh day is a day of rest, dedicated to me."

09 The Ten Commandments

God told Moses, "In six days, I made the Earth, the sky, the sea, and everything in them, but on the seventh day I rested. That is why I, the Lord, blessed the Sabbath and made it holy." God then gave ten commandments, to be followed by the Israelites. The Ten Commandments are:

"I am the Lord, your God. You shall have no other God.

You shall not make any idol of mine to worship.

You shall not take the name of the Lord in vain.

Always remember the Sabbath day.

Honour your father and your mother.

You shall not kill.

You shall not commit adultery.

You shall not steal.

You shall not lie.

You shall not covet."

God wrote these laws on two tables of stone with His own finger. He told Moses to take it down to the Israelists. If they wanted to please God, they were to always remember and follow these laws all their lives.

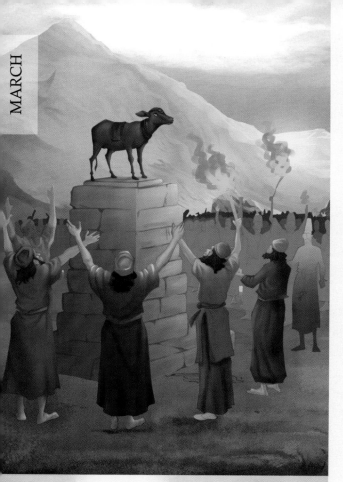

10 Disobedience

Moses stayed up on the mountain listening to God. Tired of waiting for Moses to come down, the people gathered around Aaron complaining, "We do not know what has happened to Moses. Let us make an idol of our God!"

Afraid of what the people would do, Aaron commanded them to bring gold and he made a golden calf! The delighted Israelites began to dance and joyfully shout, "This is the God that brought you out of Egypt!"

The next day, they offered sacrifices to it, sat down to eat, drink and play. They organised a festival of worship. The dancing and clapping began.

"It's not really a party for us," the children muttered, and they hid under tables. God and God's laws had been forgotten.

11 Obedience

God saw what was happening. He was angry. He sent Moses down. Moses came down the mountain carrying with him the two stone tables with God's laws. When he heard the sound of the singing and dancing, he was very angry. When he saw the golden calf, he flung the stone tables at the foot of the mountain and they broke. Moses ground the calf to powder, mixed it in water and made the Israelites drink it. Then he went back to God asking for forgiveness.

God told Moses to cut two new stone tablets and said that the agreement with the people could be renewed. God said, "I, the Lord, am a God who is full of compassion and pity, who is not easily angered and who shows great love and faithfulness. I keep my promise for thousands of generations and forgive evil and sin."

12 Making Things Right

God saw the Israelites commit sins and was very angry. Moses asked God to punish him for the people's sins. But God said that each one would have to answer for his own sins.

God taught Moses how the Israelites can atone for sins they committed. He instructed that the wrong doers can bring a sheep or bull and sacrifice it at the altar outside Tabernacle. The wrongdoers can bring grain, oil and flour as gifts to God. God told Moses that if the wrongdoers followed His instructions, then He will forgive them. Only if the Israelites followed every law laid down by Him, then only God will keep his promise to lead them across the desert to the Promised Land. Moses passed the laws and the instructions laid down by God to his people and they did as they were told. Soon, they packed their belongings to set out towards the Promised Land.

13 A Place to Worship

Before Moses came down from the Mount Sinai, with God's Ten Commandments, God said, "Make a special tent—a tabernacle—for the Israelites to worship me."

God gave specific instructions to Moses about how to build a special tent. God told Moses that the tent was to be made of ten curtains of same size, made of white linen and sewn with blue, scarlet and purple yarn. The curtains was to have pictures of cherubim painted on it and hooked up on wooden structures with golden hooks. The whole structure was to be covered with goat's hair and sheepskin, fastened with bronze clasps. Moses knew that collecting the raw materials, as the Israelites had the gold, silver and cloth from Egypt and decided to give the responsibility to the best crafts man in the camp to make the tabernacle.

14 God's Holy Tent

When Moses came down from Mount Sinai and gave the commandments to the Israelites, he called the master-craftsman Bezaleel and gave him the responsibility to set up the tabernacle. The Israelites were very generous and gave all the gold and silver they had carried from Egypt for the tabernacle.

15 First Look into Canaan

The Israelites and Moses continued their journey from Mount Sinai and reached a settlement Kadesh. Moses knew that they were near Canaan and wanted to know about the land. He sent twelve men, to check if the land was fertile or not. The men went away and came back after forty days, carrying fruits as a proof that the land was really fertile. The men said, "The land is very fertile indeed. But the men are so tall and muscular! How will fight with those giants?" Only Caleb and Joshua said, "God is with us." God was angry that the Israelites doubted His words and told Moses, "The men who doubted me will never see the promised land, neither will their children. They will wander in the desert for forty years. Only Caleb and Joshua and their children, will get to see the promised land."

16 Moses Gets Angry

The Israelites were not happy to wander in the desert for so long. When they got thirsty, they complained to Moses and blamed him. Moses turned to God, who told him, "I will guide you to a rock, strike the rock with your staff, and water will come gushing out."

Moses took the Israelites to the rock, guided by God. He was very angry with their constant complaints of the Israelites and out of anger, struck the rock twice with his staff. Water came gushing out of the rocks, but God was very angry with Moses and said, "Because you did not follow my word and became very angry, you will not lead your people to Canaan."

Moses was really sad, but accepted God's punishment. Over the years, he lost his sister Miriam and his brother Aaron, which made him sad but he continued to guide the Israelites in the desert and kept their belief in God.

17 The Israelites' Discontent

The Israelites continued their long journey. They came from Mount Hor by the way of the Red Sea. But the people were very sad. They were growing very tired of walking and wandering around in the desert and wilderness. They kept complaining.

They had hoped to see the Promised Land but now they could not see the Land anywhere. All they saw was more and more sandy desert. Angrily, they turned towards Moses and shouted, "Why did you bring us here, Moses? There is no bread or water. And we are tired of eating manna."

At this, God got angry. He had always taken care of his people, but they were never satisfied. So God sent fiery snakes into their camp. The snakes bit many people and several died that day.

18 Moses and the Brass Serpent

The Israelites did not stop complaining to Moses about the difficulties they faced every day. God heard their complaints and became very angry. He sent poisonous snakes to the Israelite camp as a punishment. The snake bit many people and some even died. The people approached Moses and asked him to pray to God to end the punishment. Moses prayed to God and He gave him a solution. Moses approached the Israelites and said, "Model a snake out of bronze and put it up on a pole. Anyone, who gets bitten by a snake will have to look at the bronze snake and he will be healed."

The Israelites followed God's order and put a bronze snake on a pole in the middle of the camp. Whoever got bitten would look at the bronze snake and was healed. God was happy with the renewed faith of the people.

19 Moses's Last Moments

The Israelites travelled in the desert for many years and Moses realised that it was time for them to enter Canaan, the Promised Land. But Moses also remembered that God had said that he will not lead the Israelites to Canaan. Thus, he went to the Israelites and said, "I am hundred and twenty years old and as God had said, I will not be able to lead you to the Promised Land. Thus, I appoint Joshua to lead you to Canaan. God has taken care of you till now and will always stay with you. He will never abandon you."

Moses turned to Joshua and said, "You must lead your people to Canaan, the Promised Land and divide it amongst them fairly. God will give you guidance and help you in your journey."

20 The Laws

After giving Joshua the responsibility to lead the Israelites to Canaan, Moses went to the tabernacle to pray. God said to Moses, "Your time is near and you shall now join your ancestors. I will lead my people to Canaan as promised. But they will divide and adopt other gods. Thus, I want you to write down everything I have told you."

Moses did exactly what God had wanted him to do and wrote down everything in a book. He took the books to the Levites (the people who were responsible to carry the Ark of Covenant) and told them to keep the book in the tabernacle, near the scared chest.

He addressed the Israelites one last time, before he left. He said, "Believe in our God, as he is just, true and right." He blessed the twelve tribes of Israel and gave special attention to Joseph's tribe as Joseph was considered 'a prince among his brothers'.

21 The Death of Moses

God told Moses to climb Mount Nebo, which was near River Jordan in Jericho. The fertile land, cities and rivers could be seen from there. God spoke to Moses, "See the land that was promised to the children of Abraham, Isaac and Jacob. See the land before you die."

Moses was very happy to see Canaan, even if it was from a distance. He and his people had suffered a lot to reach the Promised Land. He died on the mountain overlooking Canaan. The Israelites gave him a proper funeral and buried him in the nearby valley.

22 Balak's Message for Balaam

When the Israelites settled down near Canaan and stared defeating various tribes, the Moabites were alarmed. Their king, Balak, contacted the nearby tribes to create an army and defeat the Israelites. He sent a messenger to a wise man, Balaam, asking him to come and help them by cursing the Israelites.

That night, God came in Balaam's dream and said, "You shall not curse my people. They have my blessings." The next morning, he sent a word to Balak saying that he won't be able to help him. When Balak insisted, Balaam prayed to God and asked him for guidance. God said, "Go, if you must. But, you will have to follow all my commands."

Balaam agreed and set out to Moab the very next day, on his donkey.

23 Balaam and his Talking Donkey

Balaam set out to Moab to help King Balak. During the journey, the donkey suddenly changed its course and trotted on a different route. Balaam beat the donkey with a stick, but the donkey didn't correct his course.

After some time, the donkey refused to walk between two stone walls. Balaam beat the donkey again. Then the donkey suddenly sat down on the road. The donkey said, "Why are beating me up? I am just following God's orders. You cannot see the angel but I can."

Balaam looked where the Donkey was looking and saw an angel. The angel said, "I tried to stop you, but you insist on reaching your destination. You may continue this journey, only if you promise to say as God wishes." Balaam agreed to the condition and continued on his journey.

24 Balaam and King Balak

King Balak was very happy to see Balaam and welcomed him graciously. They discussed about their plan to curse the Israelites and King Balak gave orders to get everything prepared. Soon, the seven altars for animal sacrifices were prepared.

But when Balaam stepped forward to place the curse on the Israelites, he could only utter, "How can I curse the people who are blessed by God?" King Balak was furious, but insisted that Balaam tries again. When Balaam tried again, he said, "I cannot place a curse on God's blessed people." King Balak tried to convince Balaam with various riches, but Balaam could not place a curse on Israelites. Instead, he blessed the Israelites, making King Balak angrier.

25 Rahab and the Israelites

After Moses died, God spoke to Joshua and said, "Follow my word and I will guide you." Before taking over Canaan, he sent two spies who scaled the walls of Jericho and entered Canaan. Rahab, whose house was near the wall, saw the spies and called them inside. She told them that if they are caught, they will be hanged. Saying so, she hid them on her roof, behind a pile of hay. Suddenly the soldiers of Canaan knocked on her door, asking her if she had seen any Israelites. Rahab said, "I saw them leave the gates when the doors were being shut."

The soldiers went away and Rahab, gave the spies a rope to help them escape. Before the spies left, she said, "Remember the kindness I showed you and spare my family when you come to conquer." The spies agreed and said, "Bring your family in this house and tie a red thread on your window. Your house will be spared."

26 Joshua Prays for Guidance

Joshua was daunted by the responsibility to lead the Israelites to a war to Canaan. He remembered what Moses had told him, and he prayed to God for guidance. God spoke to Joshua, "I shall guide you to win the war and conquer Canaan. It is the land that I had promised your ancestors and I shall be with you. Follow my instructions and you will lead my people to the land."

Joshua believed in God and vowed to follow the instructions given by Him. Joshua's ancestors had suffered a lot to reach the Promised Land and he decided that he will fulfil his responsibility towards the Israelites.

27 Crossing the River

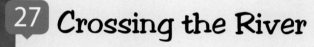

The spies returned from Jericho and told Joshua that the people in Jericho are fearing an invasion from the Israelites. Joshua realised that it was time to attack and prayed to God for guidance. God gave him instructions to cross the river.

The next day Joshua spoke to the ones who carried the Ark of Covenant and told them to walk ahead of the people, to Jericho. Then, Joshua gathered priests and soldiers to cross the River Jordan and invade Jericho. The people carrying the ark led the army of Israelites near River Jordan. As soon as they stepped in to the river, the water suddenly became still and dry land appeared underneath their feet. The Israelites rejoiced to see the strip of dry land in the river. They crossed the river easily and turned to Joshua for further instructions.

59

28 Crossing River Jordan

As soon as the Israelites crossed River Jordan, Joshua asked them to settle down for the night and wait for God's instructions. The water in the River Jordan started flowing again. Joshua chose twelve people from the twelve tribes and asked them to pick up a stone from the river bed and create a pillar, to thank God.

Suddenly, a man carrying a sword approached them and demanded to speak to Joshua. He told Joshua how God wanted them to invade Jericho in seven days. Joshua went to the camp and gathered the priests to tell them the plan. The next morning, the Israelites carried the ark around the walls of Jericho and the priests followed the ark blowing horns and trumpets. The gates had been sealed and the people of Jericho stayed in fear of what the Israelites would do. The Israelites carried out the routines for six days.

29 Into Canaan

The Israelites circled the walls of the city of Jericho, carrying the ark followed by the Israelite priests blowing their horns and trumpets. The gates to the city of Jericho were shut and the people of Jericho sat in anxiety, waiting for the Israelites to attack. On the seventh day, the ark was bought and kept in front of the gate, and the priest gathered around it and blew their horns and trumpets.

The walls protecting the city from invasion came crumbling down and the Israelite soldiers entered the city and attacked. Some soldiers went to Rahab's house and rescued everyone in the house, and smuggled them to safety. The Israelites fought bravely.

30 Gibeonites Trick Joshua

The people from the city of Gibeon heard about the way Joshua had defeated Jericho. So they decided to trick the Israelites. They gathered old wineskins and put on the backs of their animals to make it look as if they had travelled from far away. The men put on old clothes. Then they went to the camp of the Israelites and said, "We have travelled from a faraway country. We want to make an agreement with you."

Joshua asked, "Who are you? Where do you come from?" The men answered, "We are your servants. We have come from a faraway country. We came because we heard of the great power of your God."

Joshua agreed to make peace with them. He agreed to let them live.

31 Joshua Helps Gibeonites

Three days later, the Israelites learned that these men lived very near their camp. So the Israelites went to the place where they lived. On the third day, the Israelites came to the cities of Gibeon, Kephirah, Beeroth and Kiriath Jearim. But the army of Israel did not try to fight against those cities. They had made a peace agreement with them. All the people complained against the leaders who made the agreement but the leaders answered, "We have given our promise. We cannot hurt them or God will be angry with us because we broke the promise we made to them."

So the leaders did not break their promise. Joshua called the Gibeonites together and they became slaves, but Joshua let them live. He did not allow the Israelites to kill them. He made them slaves of the Israelites.

01 Complete Conquest of Canaan

After defeating the Amorites, the Israelites led by Joshua defeated many cities and conquered Canaan. The Israelites conquered thirty-one cities and defeated the mighty armies of tribes of Jericho to Tirzah.

Thus, after a long struggle of slavery, banishment and war, Israelites finally settled down in Canaan, the Promised Land. They made the Gibonites their slaves and Joshua made sure that no harm comes to them.

Israelites took over the running of Canaan, expertly supervised by Joshua who kept his promise of leading the Israelites to Canaan and believing in God. Till the end of his life, he encouraged the belief of God in people and reminded them of the various miracles God performed.

02 Dividing the Land

God told Joshua to cast lots and divide the land among all the twelve tribes of Israel. All the Israelites had descended from Jacob's twelve sons. Their own names became the tribe names! They were Reuben, Simeon, Levi, Judah, Issachar, Zebulun, Dan, Naphtali, Gad, Asher and Benjamin. Joseph was not a tribe, but his sons, Manasseh and Ephraim, became two tribes! God separated the tribe of Levi to Himself to be His priests. They were to actively maintain the house and work of God, and teach the Israelites His law. So, they did not get any land.

God made sure that Levi would have enough to live on! Each of the eleven tribes would give them one part out of every ten parts they earned! Even today, giving one-tenth of our income to God is still practised.

03 Deborah Helps Barak

Israel had no leader after Joshua died and soon people began to worship idols. So judges were chosen to ask God and advice those who came to them. Deborah, a prophetess, sat under a palm tree and judged Israel.

Jabin, King of Canaan along with Sisera, his commander, troubled Israel for twenty years. One day, Deborah told Barak, "God is going to help us win Sisera. Go and collect ten thousand soldiers for battle, from Naphtali and Zebulun." But Barak asked Deborah to come with him! Deborah agreed.

Then Deborah commanded, "Go forward. Today, God will make you defeat, Sisera!"

God went before Barak and troubled Sisera's army by sending rain. Every single soldier was killed. Sisera jumped off his chariot and ran away! God helped Israel win a great victory!

63

04 Jael and Sisera

Barak had won the battle with Deborah's help. But he had to find Sisera. Sisera left his chariot and ran towards his city, Hazor. Suddenly, he saw some tents of a tribe friendly with King Jabin. Sisera saw Jael, the wife of Heber, standing at the doorway of her tent. Jael kindly invited Sisera inside.

When Sisera gratefully stepped in, Jael made him lie down. "Please give me some water!" Sisera asked. Jael opened a bottle of milk for him.

He drank it and lay down. Jael covered him and he went off to sleep. Jael quietly took a hammer and a long nail. Silently, she came near the sleeping soldier. With one swift blow, she hammered the nail right through Sisera's temple. It went through his head pinning him to the ground. When Barak came looking for Sisera and saw the dead man, Barak was happy. Israel was free.

05 God Chooses Gideon

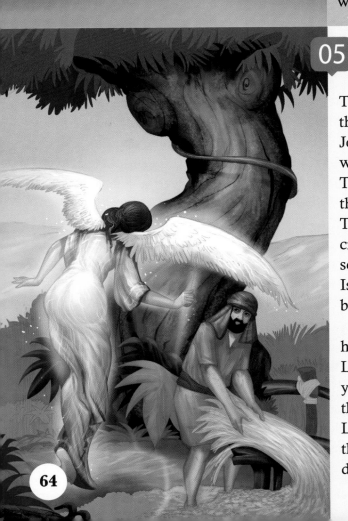

The people of Israel had promised Joshua that they would be faithful to their God. But, after Joshua died, many of them were drawn to worshipping other gods. They forgot the laws. Thus, God let the people of Midian rule over them. These were a fierce people of the desert. They rode on camels and destroyed the Israelites' crops and stole their flocks of animals. For seven harvest seasons, the Midianites invaded Israel on camelback and stolen everything. Israel became poor.

One day, Gideon was threshing the wheat he had harvested. Suddenly, the Angel of the Lord appeared, saying, "The Lord is with you!" Gideon said, "If God is with us, why this suffering? No, God has forgotten us!" The Lord said, "You are going to save Israel from the Midianites!" The Lord promised to help him defeat the Midianites.

06 The Stories of the Heroes

Gideon got some freshly made broth in a pot, bread in a basket and some meat. He placed it on a rock. The Angel touched it with his staff and fire rose up from the rock.

That night, Gideon destroyed his father's altar with the idol of Baal, as God had commanded. The whole community was angry when they saw what had happened. They wanted to punish Gideon.

"Bring us Gideon!" they shouted, "he will pay for his action with his life."

"Let Baal defend himself," shouted Gideon's father. "It was his altar."

The so-called God worked no wonders. Suddenly uncertain, the people stopped shouting. Gideon re-established the worship.

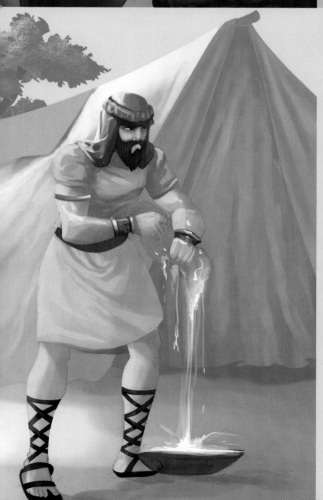

07 Gideon Checks with God

Gideon prayed, "Oh! God, please give me a sign that You have chosen me. I will place this fleece tonight on the floor. In the morning when I check it, if I find the fleece is wet with dew but the ground around it is dry, I will surely know that You have chosen me."

The next morning, when Gideon checked, the fleece was so wet that he could squeeze a bowlful of water from it! But the ground was dry! Gideon was very happy but still unsure. He begged God, "Please do not be angry with me. Show me once more that you have chosen me. This time let the ground be wet with dew, and the fleece alone stay dry."

God answered Gideon's prayer. When Gideon checked the next morning it was exactly so! Gideon was then truly ready.

08 God Picks Gideon's Army

First, God told Gideon to gather an army. The army had 32,000 people but God said the army was too big! God knew that with such a large army the Israelites would claim that it was themselves, in their own strength, and not the Lord, who had defeated the Midianites!

So God told Gideon to send all those who were afraid, straight home! 22,000 soldiers returned home. God said, "There are still too many men in the army!" This time God asked Gideon to watch the two ways in which people drank water and Gideon chose those who scooped up the water in their palms. Finally, Gideon's army had only 300 men. "Do not fear, Gideon," God promised, "with these 300 men, you will win great victory over the Midianites!"

09 Gideon Overhears the Midianites

Gideon and his army were sleeping. The Midianites were camped in the valley below them. That night, God said, "Gideon, go now into the Midianite camp. I have delivered them into your hands. Go quietly down into the camp and hear them talking. Take your servant, Purah."

So Gideon and his servant crawled down into the Midianite camp. Finally, he overheard two people, "I had a dream," said one Midianite, "I saw a small cake of barley bread tumble and land in our camp, right on to one of our tents. The tent simply fell flat!" The other man replied, "This means that God has given the Midianite army into the hands of Gideon!" Delighted and encouraged, Gideon gratefully worshipped God and returned to camp. He woke up his men and told them, "The Lord has given us the Midianites. Come, let us go defeat them!"

10 Gideon and the Midianites

Gideon trusted God, although his army was small. God told them to take only a trumpet and an empty pitcher with a lamp under it! Gideon divided them into three groups of one hundred each and approached the Midianite camp from three directions! Gideon instructed them, "Whatever you see me do, do exactly the same! When I blow the trumpet, all of you blow your trumpets! Then shout, 'The Sword of the Lord and of Gideon!'"

As the Midianites slept, Gideon's three bands approached them from three sides! At Gideon's command, they blew their trumpets and broke the pitchers revealing the light. Then they shouted, "The sword of the Lord and of Gideon!" The Midianite army woke up! Seeing the lights all around them and hearing the trumpets and Gideon's men shouting, they panicked. They fought each other in the dark while some fled! God gave Gideon victory without striking a blow!

11 Jephthah's Thoughtless Promise

Soon the Israelites forgot God again! This time the Ammonites attacked them. They needed a leader. They found Jephthah, a brave man whose half-brothers had driven him away from home. The elders of Gilead begged Jephthah to help them. He said, "If I lead you to victory, then I will return to Gilead as a leader!"

The Gileadites agreed. Jephthah foolishly promised God, "If we win the battle, I will sacrifice the first living thing I see when I return home!"

Jephthah won! When he reached home, his only daughter came running to meet him. He told her about his promise to God. His daughter begged him, "Please give me some time and then you can fulfill your promise."

Jephthah agreed, but God never expects such sacrifices, which he had already told Abraham.

12 A Special Baby is Promised

The Israelites again forgot God. So God allowed the Philistines to trouble them for 40 years. One day, the Angel of the Lord appeared to Manoah's wife. He said she would soon have a baby. But he warned her to never drink wine, eat grapes or any food 'unclean' by God's law. The child would be a Nazarite from birth, meaning they should never cut his hair. He would save Israel from their enemies.

Manoah prayed, "Please God, send the messenger again to tell us how to raise the child."

The Angel revisited them. Manoah quickly brought some meat offering and placed it on a rock. Fire rose from the offering and the Angel went up in the flame.

They called the baby Samson and God's Spirit was upon the child.

13 Samson the Strong

Samson grew so strong that no one could defeat him. The Philistines wanted to destroy him.

The Philistines heard that Samson spent a lot of time with Delilah. The Philistines told Delilah that they would each give her 1,100 pieces of silver if she discovered the secret of Samson's strength.

Then on, Delilah troubled Samson to tell her his secret. Samson said that if he were tied with green bowstrings he would become weak. When he slept, Delilah tied him with the bowstrings. "Samson, the Philistines have come!" she said. He awoke, snapping the bowstrings like thread! Delilah pleaded, "Tell me your secret." Then Samson said if she tied him with unused ropes, he would become weak. Delilah did just that. "Wake up, Samson, the Philistines are here!" This time, too, Samson broke the ropes easily and got up!

14 Samson's Secret

Delilah was very angry as she wanted to know Samson's secret. Delilah cried, "Do not mock me like this!"

Then Samson said that he would lose his strength if his hair were woven in a loom and fixed with a pin. Delilah tried this, too. Samson again pulled free with one movement! The Philistines were unhappy because Delilah could not find Samson's secret. Delilah was angry with Samson for cheating her three times. She troubled and worried him so much that Samson became really tired of it.

Finally, he told her, "I am a Nazarite from birth. My hair has never ever been cut. If it is cut, then I will surely become weak."

This time Delilah knew that Samson was telling her the truth and she at once, sent for the Philistines.

15 Samson's Defeat

When Delilah called them, the Philistines came eagerly with the money in their hands!

Then Delilah made Samson sleep. She quickly called for a man to shave off Samson's seven locks of hair. Then she called out, "Samson, wake up, the Philistines are upon you!" Samson awoke, not realising that God's Spirit had left him.

He tried to resist the Philistines as before, but he could not.

The Philistines took hold of him. They mocked him and blinded him. Then they brought him to Gaza. There, they chained him with brass fetters and made him grind the grain in the prison house. Samson had not honoured God's great gift. He had a lot of time to think and repent for his mistake while he was in the prison.

The Philistines rejoiced when Samson was captured. They celebrated a feast to their God Dagon, praising him for delivering their enemy into their hands!

16 Samson's Final Victory

During the feast the Philistines decided to call Samson. Meanwhile, in prison, Samson's hair grew. A young boy led Samson into the temple of Dagon. They placed him between two pillars. They were praising their God.

Samson asked the boy, "Please put my arms around the pillars supporting this temple!" The boy helped him.

Then, Samson pleaded with the God of Israel, "God please remember me. Strengthen me only one more time. Let me punish these Philistines for blinding my eyes."

Holding the pillars with his outstretched arms, Samson bowed himself down with all his might. God graciously returned Samson's strength. The pillars supporting the temple crashed, bringing the whole building down.

17 Naomi

In Israel's history there is a tale about a foreign woman who agreed to worship the God of Israel and was blessed.

Long ago, there was a great famine. A man named Elimelech travelled with his wife and sons from the city of Bethlehem to the country of Moab. While they were there, the man died. His two sons grew up and each married a girl from Moab. Some years later, the sons died and Elimelech's widow, Naomi, was left to live with her daughters-in-laws.

Time passed and Naomi heard that there were once again good harvests in her homeland. She decided to return. "You girls, return to your homes," she said to her daughters-in-laws.

"May the Lord help each of you to find a new husband from among your own people."

18 The Story of Ruth

When Naomi asked her daughters-in-laws to go, one of them, Ruth, refused to leave her.

Ruth said, "Please do not ask me to leave you. Where you go, I will go. Where you live, I will live. Your God shall be my God. Your people shall be my people. May God judge me if I leave you. Only death shall separate us!"

Naomi was very happy that Ruth was coming with her. When the two women reached Bethlehem, barley was being harvested.

"Let me go to the fields," said Ruth, "I will gather the grain that the harvesters leave behind."

While she worked, the owner of the fields came by. His name was Boaz and he was a relative of Naomi.

"Who is that young woman?" he asked one of his men. "She is the foreign girl who has returned from Moab with Naomi."

19 Ruth and Boaz

When Boaz saw Ruth in his field, he went to her. He heard her story and felt sorry. He told her not to go to any other field. He gave her food and water. He also told the reapers not to trouble her and to drop some extra grain for her to pick!

One day, Naomi advised Ruth to go and lie down at Boaz's feet when he was sleeping near the heap of grain. Ruth obeyed.

Boaz woke up surprised to see Ruth asleep at his feet! He sent her home with some barley. Then, he consulted relatives and finally, bought Naomi's husband's property.

Later, Boaz asked the elders of the city permission to marry Ruth.

God blessed Boaz and Ruth with a son, Obed, who was the grandfather of King David! So Ruth, who was not an Israelite, became part of the family line in which Jesus Himself was born.

20 The Story of Samuel-I

As the years passed, the Israelites grew weary of the cycle of prosperity and disaster that matched their times of obedience and disobedience to God. Eventually, they cried out to be given a king who would rule them. The accounts of that time begin with the story of the nation's last judge, Samuel.

In the place called Shiloh there was a little temple. Every year, those who were faithful to God travelled there to offer sacrifices. Every year, a man, Elkanah, visited the temple in Shiloh to worship God. One year, Hannah accompanied her husband. She was very sad because she had no children. Elkanah was kind to her.

Then Hannah went to the temple to pray. Eli, a priest, sitting in in the temple, was watching Hannah.

21 Hannah's Prayer

When Hannah was praying in the temple, a priest was watching her. Her heart was so heavy that she began to cry and pray.

She said, "God, please look upon me with kindness and bless me with a son, I promise I will give him back to you all the days of his life. I shall not let his hair be cut at all. He shall be separated for your service."

Although not a sound came from her mouth, she kept moving her lips.

Eli heard her explanation and blessed her, "May God bless you and grant you your desire!"

Hannah left the temple rejoicing that God would give her a son.

22 The Story of Samuel-II

The next year, Hannah had a baby. She called him Samuel. Hannah left him with Eli in Shiloh. Samuel served in the temple. One night, while Samuel slept, God called him by name.

Samuel thought Eli had called him. But when he asked Eli, he said he had not! When the same thing happened a third time, Eli told Samuel that God was calling him.

Samuel said, "Your servant is listening!"

God told Samuel that He was going to punish Eli's sons. Samuel would be His priest and serve Him faithfully.

The next morning, Samuel opened the doors of the temple. Eli asked Samuel what God had said. Samuel told Eli that God was going to judge his house. Eli was sad. Samuel continued in the temple, serving God. Everyone knew Samuel would become a great prophet of God.

23 Samuel Seeks a King

Samuel led the people wisely. He travelled around the country, encouraging people to stay faithful to God and helped in settling disputes with his good judgements. But Samuel's sons did not follow his good example.

In those days, Israel was ruled by judges, not kings. But when Samuel was old, the Israelites wanted a king! Samuel said that a king would take their sons to do his field work and make weapons of war; he would make them his soldiers. The girls would become cooks and bakers. A tenth of their produce and their vineyards would be his! Their cattle and livestock, too he would not spare!

Yet the people insisted!

God was sad. He had been Israel's King, but He told Samuel to give them a king. God told Samuel He had chosen a king from the tribe of Benjamin, who Samuel would meet the next day.

24 Samuel Meets the King

In the region of Zuph, crowds gathered on a hilltop to offer sacrifices to great prophet Samuel, to arrive and lead the ceremony.

Samuel was on his way when he heard footsteps of two men approaching him. One was clearly a servant; the other, taller and remarkably handsome, had the appearance of a rich man's son.

"I am looking for the prophet," said the taller of the two, "can you tell me where he lives?"

"I am he," replied Samuel and all at once he felt that God's message had come true.

"Go ahead to the place of worship on the hill. Then stay and eat with me this evening."

"We haven't come here for that," said the men.

"Tomorrow I will answer your questions," said Samuel. Then he smiled at them, for he knew with absolute certainty what he needed to say.

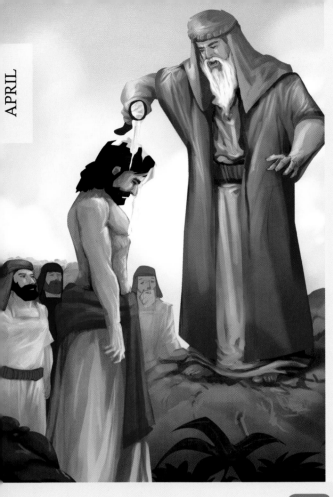

25 Saul

Samuel said to the men, "I know you are looking for donkeys that have been lost. They have already been found."

The young man and his servant were surprised. How did the prophet know their business? "And you," Samuel went on, addressing the rich young man, "you are the one that the people of Israel are seeking."

"What do you mean?" The handsome youth was suddenly embarrassed and nervous. "I come from the smallest tribe." His voice trailed off.

Samuel had simply walked on ahead. The next day, Samuel took a jar of olive oil and performed a simple ceremony. He poured the oil on to the head of the tall young man. "Saul," he said to him, "the Lord has chosen you to be the ruler of his people." On that day, Saul knew that God was leading him.

26 The Great Kings

Days passed. The young men returned home to a household where everything in their quiet world seemed to be as normal.

Just as their adventure was fading to memory, an announcement came that all the people of Israel should gather, for Samuel wished to speak to them.

Samuel had called all, Israel to Gilgal. He asked each tribe to step forward, for he was going to select a king for them. The people paraded past. But where was the young man? Where was Saul? They found him hiding among the supplies. He was dragged out and led before the people.

"Here is the man the Lord has chosen!" cried Samuel and the people shouted, "Long live the king!"

Thus, Samuel proclaimed Saul as king. He offered sacrifices to God and they all greatly rejoiced! But Saul proved a failure and a little later Samuel had to choose another king.

27 Saul the Warrior

A month had passed since the people of Israel had welcomed Saul as their leader. However, he had come back to his father's land, working in the fields.

One day, when Saul returned home from the field, he heard weeping. "Messengers have come from the north with a message that the Ammonites have attacked them. They are begging for help."

So Saul called for volunteers to come from every tribe. Then, along with them, he marched against the enemy and won a great victory. Amid the rejoicing, Saul grew in confidence as the ruler of his people. Boldly he selected men to fight in his army. With advice from Samuel, he led them into battle against the Philistines from the west, and one victory followed another.

Strangely, there were no blacksmiths in Israel. The Philistines usually made and repaired the Israelites' weapons and farming tools.

28 Jonathan Fights with Courage

Once, during a Philistine attack, only Saul and his son, Jonathan had swords. The rest of the army was unarmed.

Jonathan told his armour bearer, "Let us climb this mountain and capture the narrow pass between the two rocks that leads to the Philistine garrison. God can save, whether we are few or many! If the Philistines say, 'Come up and fight,' we will take it as a sign that God is with us."

When the Philistines saw Jonathan and the armour bearer, they mockingly invited, "Come!"

Encouraged, they went up and killed about twenty Philistines. Suddenly, a great trembling was felt in the army. Then, Saul heard the noise in the Philistine camp growing louder. Saul and his army saw the Philistines fighting against each other! God helped Jonathan save Israel that day.

29 Saul Disobeys God

Saul was a strong and brave warrior. Even after he became king, Sameul would sometimes give him God's command and want wholeheartedly for him to carry them out.

Once, Samuel told Saul that God had commanded him to completely destroy the Amalekites, "Kill each one of them, do not spare even their cattle," he said.

Saul took a large army and came to a city in Amalek. Instead of killing them, Saul ordered the Amalekites to leave the city; else they would be destroyed.

Then Saul carried out Samuel's instructions, but he spared Agag, the king and the best cattle, both sheep and oxen.

That's how Saul disobeyed God's command and this is what led to his downfall.

30 Another Argument

When Saul disobeyed God, He told Samuel, "I regret for making Saul king! He spared Agag, the king and the best cattle, both sheep and oxen. When I told him to punish everyone."

Samuel cried all night.

Early next morning, Samuel went to see Saul and asked him about the sound of cattle. Saul said, "We saved the best cattle to sacrifice to the Lord!"

Samuel said, "No, Saul, to obey is better than sacrifice. God is displeased with you. He will give the kingdom to a better man. Rebellion is like witchcraft and stubbornness is like idolatry in God's sight!"

31 Samuel Chooses a New King

The Israelites moved from Mount Sinai towards Canaan, but the rulers of Canaan, the Philistines, refused to let the Israelites settle. The conquest of Canaan went on for many years. When King Saul was the king of the Israelites, God asked the high priest Samuel, "Choose for Me a king, from among the sons of Jesse, a shepherd who lives in Bethlehem."

In Bethlehem, Samuel offered a sacrifice to God. Samuel purified all those who came. Jesse and his sons came, too. Samuel knew that God had chosen one of Jesse's sons, but he did not know which one! So as the first son walked up to him, Samuel admired his height, strength and build!

But then, in his thoughts, he heard the clear voice of God, "I do not judge as people judge. They look at the outward appearance, but I look at the heart." So, Samuel kept looking till he found the chosen one.

79

01 David is the New King

After Jesse's seven sons had walked past Samuel and God had not shown Samuel who was the king, Samuel was puzzled. He asked Jesse if he had any more sons! Jesse's youngest son, David, was looking after his father's sheep. Samuel asked Jesse to send for him. David came running, with his homemade harp swinging from his shoulder. He was a good looking, strong, young man.

God told Samuel that this was the new king. He had chosen! So, Samuel took his horn of oil and anointed David in front of his brothers. From then on the Spirit of God rested upon David. Samuel returned to the city of Ramah. With the future of the kingdom secure, Samuel lived his days on the fringes of Saul's kingdom. But, David had to wait many long and difficult years before he actually became king.

02 David and his Harp

After God chose David to be king, He sent a spirit to trouble King Saul who became very disturbed.

Saul's servants suggested that they find a talented harp player who would play music to dispel the evil spirit. They suggested Jesse's son, David, who was a skilled harpist.

Saul was pleased. He asked Jesse to send David to the palace. Jesse sent David with some bread, a bottle of wine and a goat as gifts for Saul.

Soon, David became one of Saul's favourite subjects. Whenever Saul was troubled, David played the harp and calmed him down.

03 The Giant Goliath

Time passed and soon there was another war with the Philistine army. King Saul was very worried. His army had camped all around him on a hillside. On the other side of the hill, the Philistine army was cheering. Saul was very sad as he knew he could not defeat the Philistine army this time. He saw two soldiers, from the enemy camp, walk towards them. One was a giant man, clad in gleaming bronze and wielding a massive spear. The other soldier walked in front of him carrying his shield.

"Slaves of Saul," shouted the giant, Goliath, "I dare you to pick someone to fight me. Beat me, and the whole army will surrender to you!" No one answered the challenge, as no one had the courage to face the giant alone.

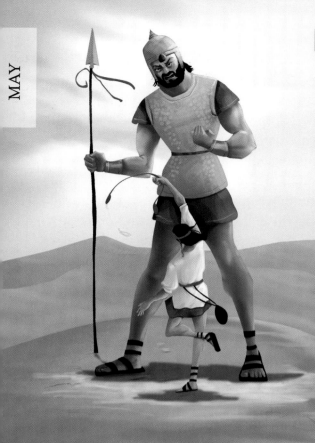

04 David and Goliath

When David went to meet his brothers in King Saul's army, he saw Goliath at the enemy camp and loudly exclaimed, "I will go and defeat this giant!"

King Saul said, "You are but a boy. I cannot let you go!" David replied "King, I have killed a lion and a bear with my bare hands, while protecting my father's sheep. God was with me then and He will be with me now!"

King Saul gave his permission. David did not wear armour or carry a sword. He just picked up five smooth stones from the brook for his slingshot. As David went towards him, Goliath laughed and said, "You, little man, will fight me?"

David swung his slingshot and the pebble struck Goliath on his forehead. Goliath fell down and David ran and cut off Goliath's head with his sword.

The Philistine army fled and the Israelites won.

05 Saul Hates David

David was a fine soldier. He soon became commander of the army. David had also become friends with Saul's son, Jonathan. People began to sing praises of David. When King Saul saw this, he was furious as he felt threatened.

The king planned to kill him. One day, when David played music to soothe King Saul's troubled spirit, he threw his spear at David. It did not hit David. He could not understand why the king was angry. Saul gave the young soldier dangerous assignments, hoping that the Philistines would kill him in battle.

David always succeeded in all that he did. Saul's daughter, Michal, fell in love with him and was delighted to be made his bride. Saul's eldest son, Jonathan, became a loyal friend and warned David of his father's schemes to kill him.

06 David and Jonathan

Jonathan, Saul's son and David were the best of friends. Jonathan promised to help David always. Jonathan asked David to promise that he would help Jonathan's family even after he became king.

Now, David and Jonathan arranged to meet in a field. Jonathan would shoot three arrows and send his servant to gather them. If Jonathan had good news he would tell the boy, "The arrows are on this side. Take them!" But if Jonathan knew that Saul was going to kill David, then he would say, "Boy! The arrows are beyond you. Go home!"

So the next day, David hid in the field. When he heard Jonathan say, "The arrows are beyond you! Go home!" David knew that Saul meant to kill him. David and Jonathan hugged each other. They made God witness to their friendship, promising to help one other's families and parted ways never to meet again.

07 David the Outlaw

Soon David was forced to live as an outlaw. In the evenings, under the stars, he still made up his own songs. "The Lord is my shepherd, I lack nothing. He makes me lie down in green pastures, he leads me beside quite waters, he refreshes my soul. He guides me along the right paths for his name's sake. Even though I walk through the darkest valley, I will fear no evil, for you are with me; your rod and your staff, they comfort me. You prepare a table before me in the presence of my enemies. You anoint my head with oil; my cup overflows. Surely your goodness and love will follow me all the days of my life, and I will dwell in the house of the Lord forever."

08 David Hides in a Cave

God saved David from wild animals. God had saved him from Goliath and although, sometimes he was driven to despair, in his heart he believed God would keep him safe always.

One day, King Saul and his soldiers came into the cave where David had been hiding. David became worried. He decided to kill King Saul but he did not. Instead, David crept towards King Saul and cut a part of his robe. When Saul left the cave, David came out, holding the torn piece of cloth. Showing it to King Saul. He said, "I had the chance to kill you, but I did not. Why do you want to kill me?"

Seeing David's conduct, Saul's anger vanished. "Oh! David, My son! You are more righteous than I am. You have rewarded me well for the evil I did to you!"

09 David Desires Water from Bethlehem's Well

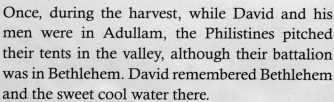

Once, during the harvest, while David and his men were in Adullam, the Philistines pitched their tents in the valley, although their battalion was in Bethlehem. David remembered Bethlehem and the sweet cool water there.

"If only I could drink water from Bethlehem's well!" David said, longingly. He did not know that his loyal men had heard him. Courageously, his three best soldiers went to Bethlehem. They forced their way through the Philistine soldiers and drew water from the well and brought it to David.

Touched by their devotion and ashamed of himself for putting them at such risk, David could not drink it. He said, "Oh Lord! Is this water not really the blood of the men whose lives I put at risk?" He poured the water as an offering before God.

10 Nabal, the Foolish Man

Samuel died and Israel mourned.

One day, David and his followers wandering in the wilderness heard about Nabal, a wealthy cattle owner was going to shear his sheep. David sent some of his followers to him.

"We have protected your cattle and shepherds. Please share your celebration with us!" they said. Nabal was foolish and selfish. "Why should I give my meat to someone I do not know?" David's men returned. Nabal's servants ran to Abigail, Nabal's wife. She quickly loaded a lot of bread, wine and sheep's meat on to some donkeys and went to meet David.

David was coming towards Nabal when he met Abigail. "Please do not be angry with Nabal," Abigail said, "His name itself means 'foolishness'. Let his sin be upon me. When the Lord makes you king, please remember me."

David blessed her, took her gifts and left.

11 The Prophesy

The victory years Saul had enjoyed were gone. His kingdom crumbled as foreign enemies closed in around him.

"To whom can I turn now, there is no prophet?" he lamented, "If only I could speak again with Samuel."

One of his advisers said, "There is a woman in Endor who claims to be able to speak with the dead," the man whispered, "I know our laws forbid it, but in moments of desperation, perhaps . . ."

"Find her for me," ordered Saul.

Among the strange shadows that flickered in the midnight hour, Saul watched as the woman conjured for him the spirit of Samuel. "Help me," pleaded Saul.

The pale figure of the prophet shook its head. "You have disobeyed the Lord," he warned, "after tomorrow's battle, you will join me beyond death's horizon."

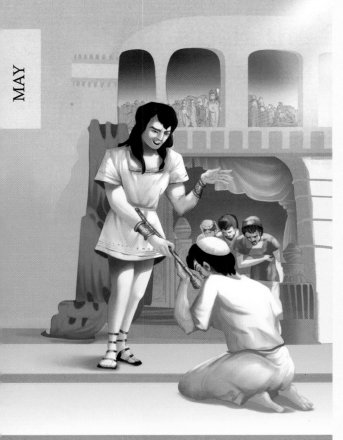

12 David is King

The dreadful prophecy came true. Saul and Jonathan were killed in a battle against the Philistines. When the news reached David, he wept in grief. Then God told David that the time had come for him to make himself king. The people from the tribe of Judah welcomed him as their leader, but others wanted a king from Saul's family.

Then followed seven years of murder and treachery. Soon, the remaining sons of Saul also died. Hence, David was made the king of all Israel. When the Philistines heard this, they decided to attack them but David proved to be a strong and clever king. He soon defeated the Philistines and drove them back.

They never dared to attack the city of God again. David decided to make Jerusalem his capital city.

13 Jerusalem, the City of God

After David became the king of the Israelites, he decided to conquer Jerusalem. Jerusalem was a flourishing and strong city, set on top of a hill. It was a fortress. Nobody could enter it easily. The people of Jerusalem did not want David to enter their city and did everything they could do to stop him.

Soon, David was able to discover underground tunnels leading into the city. One day, he sent his spies inside the city to open the gates. Then, David attacked Jerusalem by surprise. He conquered it and made it his capital city.

This is where he had his court. He ruled his kingdom from Jerusalem and made it the city of his people.

14 The Ark of the Covenant

David still did not feel satisfied. He decided that he wanted to make it the city where God resided. So, David decided to bring the Ark of the Covenant, which contained the sacred stone tablets on which the Ten Commandments were written. He knew that once the Ark was in Jerusalem, God would be with them truly.

Thus, David sent for the Ark. All the people were excited. It was brought in a great procession. Musicians played their music and people danced and sang songs. David was very happy and joined the people in the dance, in praise of the Lord.

The Ark was kept in a tent. Soon, a special place was built and the Ark was kept there and Jerusalem finally became the City of God.

15 David Plans to Build God's House

Once, David said to Nathan, the prophet, "I live in this beautiful house. I really wish I could build a wonderful house for God, too."

That night, God told Nathan that He had always lived in the Tabernacle wherever Israel had travelled but, He was pleased with David's desire.

"Tell David," God told Nathan, "I took him from the sheepfold, made him king and gave him a great name. I will continue to bless David's house and his generations, forever. I will be with his son and correct him as a father. My mercy will never leave David's house."

When Nathan told David God's words, David sat humbly before God. "Who am I Lord? What is my house that you have raised me up so high? You have promised to bless my house, forever! There is no God like you, who does great and mighty things for His people!"

87

16 David Remembers Jonathan's Family

David thought of his friendship with Jonathan. He sent a message asking if anyone from the family of Saul was still alive. Ziba, Saul's servant, told David about Jonathan's son, Mephibosheth, who lived in Lodebar. David sent for Mephibosheth, who was lame in both his feet. When he had been a child, his nurse had dropped him and he became lame. Mephibosheth bowed before David and said, "I am your servant!"

David said, "Do not fear. I will restore to you all the land that belonged to Saul. You will continually eat at the king's table with me. I do this for your father, Jonathan, my friend's sake."

Then, David told Ziba to look after Mephibosheth's land and cultivate it for him. David was happy that he had kept his promise to Jonathan.

17 David and Bathsheba

One spring, the time of year when kings often went to war, David stayed in his city while his army went to fight. Alone and with little to do, he had the leisure to sleep in the heat of the afternoon and stroll around the flat roof of the palace in the cool of the evening. One day after his nap, he saw a woman in a house not far away. She was having a bath.

David sent word to find out who she was. She was Bathsheba, the wife of Uriah, a brave soldier in David's army. David sent for her and kept her in his palace for some time. Then, she went back home. A little while later, news reached him that Bathsheba was going to have a baby. It would soon become clear that Uriah could not be the father, for he was away fighting.

18 David's Sin

Now, David did not want anyone to know about his sin. Thus, he sent for Uriah. He wanted Uriah to go to his own house and be with Bathsheba. So, everyone would think that it was their baby that would be born. But Uriah was a very good soldier. He said that he would not go home, as he was on duty. Finally, David knew that he could marry Bathsheba only after Uriah died. So, David wrote a letter to the man in charge of the fighting. "Put Uriah in the front line," he ordered, "and abandon him there."

When the news of Uriah's death was brought to Jerusalem, Bathsheba mourned. David grimly waited until the time of mourning was over. Then, David sent for Bathsheba to come to the palace and be his wife. God was angry with David for what he had done.

19 Nathan's Story

Nathan, David's prophet, visited David again to tell him a story.

"There was once a poor man who had one little lamb. It grew up along with his children, like a daughter, eating and drinking from his own hand! A very rich man lived nearby with herds and flocks. One day, when a traveller came to visit him, the rich man quickly went to the poor man's house and killed his only lamb and served him a meal."

David became furious, "If there is anyone who has really done this, he shall surely die. He shall also repay the poor man four times because he did this without pity."

Nathan said, "David, you are that man! God said that although he had anointed David as king and given him all of Israel to rule, David had valued it as too little."

89

20 David's Punishment

Nathan also said that God had told him that David had killed Uriah just to marry his wife. God said that David's wives, too, would someday face the same trouble and enemies would always rise against the house of David.

"I have sinned against the Lord," David prayed, asking for forgiveness. Nathan said that the child born to Bathsheba would die and it did. God never tolerates sin.

David wept in sorrow, and his wailing song of grief echoed through his palace.

"Be merciful to me, dear God, because of your constant love. Because of your great mercy wipe away my sins!

Create a pure heart in me, O God, and put a new and loyal spirit in me."

21 David and Absalom

David had many sons. He loved all of them dearly. As David grew old, his sons began to quarrel over who would be the next king of Israel. One day, Amnon, David's eldest son, was murdered by Absalom, his own brother. After that, Absalom fled from David, his father, and did not see him for two years. Finally, when David saw him and he kissed Absalom but he wanted to be king. So Absalom sat near the city gate and was friendly with everyone who passed through. Handsome and charming, he tried to win the people over. He said if he were made king he would see that justice was done. Then, Absalom took David's permission to go to Hebron to worship God.

He managed to raise a powerful army to defeat his father. Absalom told the people to crown him king at Hebron.

22 The Forest of Ephraim

David was angry when he heard of Absalom's actions, but he loved him too much to wish to fight back. David and his men left Jerusalem, so that the city would not be attacked and destroyed. David instructed his soldiers to defend the city at all times. But, as a loving father, he asked them never to harm Absalom. Old and tired, David hated to fight his own son.

Also, the people would not let David go to war fearing he would be killed. Thus, David divided the army under three captains. He pleaded with his captains to spare Absalom's life. The forest of Ephraim where the battle took place caused more deaths than the battle, itself!

When Absalom rode into battle on his mule, he passed under an old oak tree. His long hair got caught in the branches, leaving him dangling, helplessly.

23 Absalom's Death

While Absalom dangled, helplessly from an old oak tree, one of David's soldiers saw him. The soldier ran and told Joab, the captain.

Joab asked him why he didn't kill him.

The soldier said that he would never harm the king's son. Joab, at once, left for the place the soldier had told him. He saw Absalom hanging from the old oak tree. Joab thrust three darts through Absalom's heart and killed him. As he awaited news of the battle, David heard that they had won and that Absalom had been killed.

David was shocked. He cried, loudly, "I wish I had died instead of you, Absalom, my son." There were no celebrations, just the grief of the king.

David finally chose Solomon to ascend the throne.

24 David is King Again

Joab advised David to stop mourning and reassure the people. David sent for the priests. Soon, all the people were happy that David was again the king, whom they knew and loved. They told David, "Please return to us as king."

David then came to Jordan. The tribe of Judah, David's own tribe, met him. He arrived at his house in Jerusalem with many men from all the tribes of Israel.

David once again took over his duty as king. He collected the bones of Saul and Jonathan and buried them in Saul's hometown of Bethlehem. Till the end, he kept his promise to Jonathan, his friend. He continued to lead Israel in war. But the Israelites would not let him fight any more as he was growing old. They did not want to lose him in battle.

25 Solomon's Amazing Dream

After Bathsheba became David's wife, she bore him a second son named Solomon. He grew up learning the laws that God had given Moses. David taught him to obey God's commands.

Solomon was anointed king, when he was still a young man. Though Solomon was wise and had a good heart, he realised that he was too inexperienced to rule over Israel. Solomon decided to go to the holy place at Gibeon where he offered sacrifices to the Lord and prayed. Finally, the Lord appeared to him in a dream and said, "Solomon, I will grant you whatever you ask from Me."

"Lord, I only wish for You to give me the wisdom I need to rule your people with justice and to know the difference between good and evil," Solomon said.

26 God's Promise to Solomon

God was pleased that Solomon had asked for wisdom to rule the Israelites with justice. He promised to always answer Solomon's prayer.

God said, "When you had the chance to ask for riches, victory over your enemies or long life, you asked for wisdom. You will be unique. There will be no one like you. You will also have success and riches. You will have all of this as long as you live by my commandments. This much I will promise."

Solomon became a great king. People from all over the world visited his court. He was also a poet. The skilled writers in his court recorded thousands of his clever sayings.

He was truly a unique king.

27 Solomon the Wise

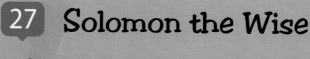

One day, two women came to Solomon's court. The first woman explained, "My Lord, we both live in the same house and each of us has a baby boy. One night, when I had put my baby to sleep, her child died. So, she came and stole my baby. In the morning, I knew that the dead baby was not mine. Now, she denies that she stole my baby."

"This baby is mine!" the second woman exclaimed. King Solomon asked his guard to cut the baby into half and give one half to each woman. The first woman flung herself at Solomon's feet.

"Please, give the baby to the other woman, but don't harm him!" she wept. The second woman said, calmly, "Of course, you can cut him."

King Solomon handed the baby to the first woman. All of Israel understood that King Solomon was indeed blessed by the Lord.

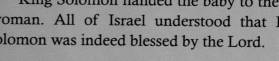

28 Solomon's Letter to Hiram

One evening, as the setting sun cast its glow over the hills of Jerusalem, Solomon sat and wrote a letter to an old friend of his father, King Hiram of Tyre, a city on the coast to the north of Israel.

"You will remember that my father, David, always wanted to build a temple here in the city of Jerusalem," he wrote, "but was unable to do so as he had so many wars to fight. Now the Lord, my God, has given me peace on all the borders of my country. I therefore wish to fulfil a promise I made to my father to build that temple. Please could you send some of your skilled woodcutters to Lebanon to cut down cedars for me. They will work alongside our people, and I will pay whatever you wish."

29 Hiram's Response

Hiram was delighted.

"I am ready to do as you ask," he replied. "My men will bring the logs from Lebanon to the sea and float them in great rafts to a port of your choosing. You can have both cedar and pine and, in return, I simply ask that you provide food for the workers."

David had brought the sacred Ark of Covenant to Jerusalem. King Solomon now was building the temple where it would be kept.

So it was that in the fourth year of Solomon's reign, four hundred and eighty years after the people of Israel left Egypt, work began on the temple.

30 Solomon's Temple

The temple took seven years to finish. It was a sight to behold. It was immense and ornate, solid and strong, yet with the finest carving and a rich gold interior. The temple was grander than any palace. The inner temple, where the Ark was to be kept, was made entirely of gold.

The day it was complete, the priests of Levi carried out a small procession, bringing the wooden chest or Ark of the Covenant inside the temple. As they left, a thick cloud of glory filled the temple.

King Solomon said, "Do not be afraid. This is the Lord's glory upon us. He has finally come to dwell in this temple!"

31 King Solomon's Prayer

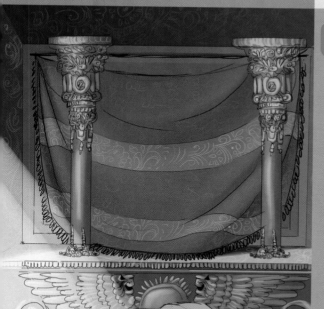

King Solomon then prayed sincerely. "Praise the Lord who has given His people peace, as He promised. He has kept all the promises He made through Moses. May the Lord be with us, as He was with our ancestors; may He never abandon us; may He make us obedient to Him, so that we always live as He wants us to, and keep all the laws and commands He gave our ancestors and so all the nations of the world will know that the Lord alone is God—there is no other."

Then God answered, "Solomon, I grant your prayer. From this day on, My Presence will remain in this temple that you have made. I will secure your throne over Israel and bless your people. But if you turn away from me, I will leave the temple, never to return."

01 Solomon in All His Glory

Solomon became rich and wise, just as God had promised. He married an Egyptian Princess, who owned a huge kingdom. He had a big army of almost one thousand four hundred chariots and twelve thousand horses. Solomon had a big navy and ships from his kingdom sailed down to the Red Sea for trade and brought back spices, gold, ivory and exotic birds.

Many caravans of camels travelled across the desert for trade. His kingdom became famous for its wealth. Solomon made himself a grand palace which took thirteen years to complete. Solomon's throne was made of ivory and overlaid with gold. It had six steps leading up to it, with two lions at the sides of the throne. Twelve lions stood, two on each side of the six steps, making it one of the most wonderful thrones ever seen. Solomon did not forget God. Solomon offered sacrifices thrice a year.

02 The Queen of Sheba Visits Solomon

One day, the Queen of Sheba visited Jerusalem to see if the stories she had heard about King Solomon's wisdom were true.

When she reached Jerusalem, she was truly amazed. When she finally met Solomon she asked him many questions. Solomon answered all questions.

The queen saw his palace, servants, the food and his magnificent throne! She said, "Everything I heard about you is true. Blessed is God for delighting in you and blessing you so much! Happy are your people; God has made you wise and your glory has spread far and wide. Your wisdom and prosperity far exceed the fame which I heard. It is because the Lord loved Israel for ever that He has made you king to mete out judgement and justice."

03 Solomon Turns Away from God

Solomon was very rich, but he spent a lot as well. He took loans to clear his debts and made people work as slaves. He had many wives from different countries, so they worshipped different gods. He made temples for their gods and started worshipping them.

God said to Solomon, "I thought you would remain faithful but because you have broken the laws of My Commandments, I will take everything away from you. For the sake of David, none of this will happen in your lifetime, but in your son's life."

When Solomon's son, Rehoboam succeeded his father, he faced many problems and Israel was divided.

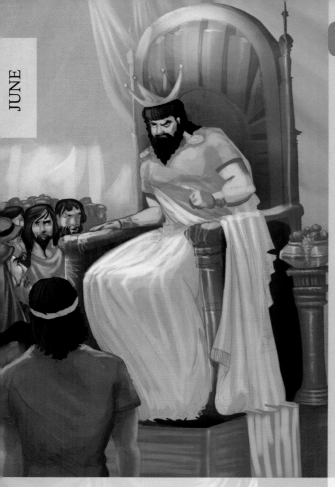

04 Rehoboam is King

The prophet, Ahijah, had said that Jeroboam would become king. But Jeroboam escaped to Egypt. After Solomon died, all Israel came to crown Rehoboam as king. Jeroboam asked Rehoboam, "King Solomon made lives difficult. If you make our burdens lighter, we will serve you!" Rehoboam replied that he would answer them after three days.

When Rehoboam asked the old men who had advised Solomon when he was king, what to do, they told him to speak kindly to the people. But Rehoboam did not listen. Rehoboam asked his friends and they advised him to be even harsher than Solomon had been. Rehoboam was pleased. Rehoboam told the people, "My father made your burdens heavy; I will make them heavier. He punished you with only whips; I will whip you with scorpions!" Angry and hurt, Israel refused to obey Rehoboam as king.

05 Jeroboam is the Next King

Rehoboam was angry and he sent Adoram, the man in-charge of tax collection, to punish the ten tribes of Israel but the people stoned him to death!

Israel then crowned Jeroboam as king. Rehoboam had only the tribes of Judah and Benjamin to rule over. Now, God's people were divided into the northern kingdom of Israel and the southern kingdom of Judah. Jeroboam thought that if the people went to Jerusalem to worship God in the temple, they might rejoin Rehoboam. To stop this, Jeroboam built two gold calves in Bethel and Dan! He told Israel that these were now their gods! He himself offered upon the altar and burnt incense. God was very angry with Jeroboam. Through Prophet Ahijah, God told Jeroboam that He would punish his house for bringing idolatry into Israel.

06 The Story of the Northern Kingdom

After Jeroboam died, his son became king. But soon, Jeroboam's family was killed by others. Finally, an army officer, Omri, became the next king! Omri was very wicked. His son Ahab was the wickedest to ever rule Israel. He married Jezebel, daughter of the King of Zidon. They were Baal worshippers. Baal was the 'Bull God', the God of the rains and harvest. Now, Jezebel wanted Ahab to build an altar for Baal in Israel. She wanted Baal to be the only God to be worshipped in Israel. Thus, Ahab made the worship of Baal popular in Israel.

God was very angry with Ahab. He raised Prophet Elijah to warn Ahab of his mistakes. Elijah often bravely spoke God's words to King Ahab. But Jezebel hated Elijah and wanted to kill him.

07 Elijah at Cherith

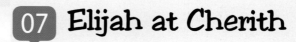

God sent prophet Elijah to King Ahab to tell him that he must end his evil ways. Elijah told Ahab that because of his wicked ways there would be no rain for three and a half years. Nothing would grow and food would become scarce. Baal was supposed to be the Rain God, so Jezebel knew Elijah was challenging Baal!

Jezebel was furious and wanted to kill Elijah. God told Elijah to hide by the Brook Cherith that flows into the Jordan. God promised Elijah, "I will send you ravens every day with bread and meat."

Obediently, Elijah hid by Brook Cherith. He drank its water and ate the food that the ravens brought him. There was no rain at all. Slowly, the brook began to dry up. Finally, God told Elijah to go to Zarephath in Zidon, where God had asked someone to look after him!

08 Elijah and the Widow

Elijah went to the city of Zidon. He was tired and hungry. At the city gate, he saw a widow gathering sticks. Elijah asked her for some water and bread.

The woman replied, "I have a handful of flour and a little oil. I am gathering these sticks to prepare the last meal. My son and I will eat it and die."

Elijah told her to bake a small cake for him first. He assured her that if she gave him that food, her flour barrel would never become empty and her oil jar would never run dry.

After cooking the meal, she discovered what Elijah had said was true. Elijah stayed with them and they never lacked food. One day, her son became ill and died. She cried bitterly.

Elijah prayed for him and he returned to life. The woman exclaimed, "I am sure that you are God's man!"

09 Elijah Returns to King Ahab

Israel's drought lasted for three and a half years. King Ahab and his servants looked for grass and water and along the dry riverbed. His fine leather sandals were not thick enough to protect him from the sharp stones, and he was angry.

He thought, *It's been three years since Elijah showed up at my court saying that there would be no rain. I can only hope that Obadiah is able to find water in the parched land!*

In the parched land, his servant, Obadiah, found Elijah and convinced him to meet the king. So Elijah visited Ahab's court and said, "You have disobeying God by worshipping Baal. Now order the people of Israel to meet me on Mount Carmel. Bring with you the prophets of Baal and of Asherah."

10 Elijah and the Fire from Heaven

The next day, the people assembled on Mount Carmel. Elijah instructed the prophets to make an altar for Baal while he made one for God.

"Let the God who is greater send fire from heaven to light the altar!" he exclaimed. The prophets of Baal started singing, dancing and praying. Yet there was no fire in their altar.

Elijah prepared his sacrifice on the altar made of twelve stones, one for every tribe of Israel. He poured water thrice on his altar till the sacrifice on it was completely soaked. He prayed, "Lord, send fire to this altar and prove today that you are indeed the true God of Israel and I am your servant!" The altar caught fire, burning up the water, the sacrifice and stones around it. All the people bowed down and acknowledged God's power. Then, Elijah killed all the false prophets of Baal at the Brook Kishon.

11 Elijah, the Champion of God

Elijah told Ahab, "Eat and drink! It will rain heavily, soon!" So, Ahab went to eat. Elijah and his servant went to the top of Mount Carmel. Elijah lay face down on the ground and asked his servant to look towards the sea and tell him what he saw.

The servant said, "I can see nothing." Elijah asked him to look seven times. The seventh time, the servant said, "There is a cloud coming out of the sea, like a man's hand!"

Elijah told the servant to tell Ahab to prepare his chariot and go down to the palace, before the rain stops him! The sky became dark and overcast! It rained after three and a half years of drought! Ahab got into his chariot and left for Jezebel. Elijah came down. God's hand was upon him. Elijah ran before Ahab's chariot all the way to the entrance of Jezebel.

12 God Speaks to Elijah

Jezebel was furious and said to Elijah, "I will make your life miserable."

Suddenly, Elijah was terrified of Jezebel. He travelled into the wilderness and cried, "Please let me die, God. It is enough!"

Elijah fell asleep. God lovingly sent an Angel. The Angel woke him, "Arise and eat. The journey is too long for you," and gave him freshly baked bread and water to drink. Elijah travelled forty days without food until he reached a cave on Mount Horeb. He told God about Jezebel's threat. A mighty wind blew, breaking the rocks into pieces. An earthquake followed, and then a fire roared.

God encouraged him to go back. He told him to anoint Jehu as king over Israel and Elisha as prophet after him.

13 Ahab and the Vineyard

A beautiful vineyard owned by Naboth was near King Ahab's palace. Ahab requested Naboth to give him his vineyard and offered to give him a better vineyard in exchange! But Naboth refused.

King Ahab became angry. Jezebel heard this and falsely accused Naboth of sin against God. Naboth was taken outside the city and stoned to death. Ahab went to the vineyard and he saw Elijah there. Elijah told Ahab that he had committed sin and God would punish both him and his wife. Ahab felt sorry for his evil doings. He took off his royal robes and wore sackcloth and went about mourning.

God was pleased that Ahab had humbly realised his mistakes and decided that he would not suffer in his own lifetime.

14 Micaiah's Prophecy

Ahab, the King of Israel, asked Jehoshaphat, the King of Judah, to help him get back the city of Ramoth from Syria. Jehoshaphat agreed, if the prophets agreed. Ahab gathered 400 prophets, who encouraged Ahab to fight. When Jehoshaphat asked for other prophets, Micaiah and Zedekiah were called.

Zedekiah, the prophet, said, "You will push the Syrians out!"

Micaiah simply said, "God will help you."

The king persisted, "Micaiah, tell us what the Lord tells you."

Micaiah said, "I see Israel scattered like sheep without a shepherd on the hills."

Micaiah said that he saw a vision where a spirit told God he would make all the prophets give Ahab the wrong message, so that Ahab would die in battle. Micaiah was imprisoned.

15 Death of Ahab

As they set out to battle, Ahab was worried. Elijah had warned Ahab that God would punish him for leading Israel into idolatry.

So, just before the battle, Ahab decided to fight wearing a disguise. Jehoshaphat wore his royal robes. The battle began. The King of Syria commanded his thirty-two captains to fight only with King Ahab. When the captains saw Jehoshaphat in his royal robes, they moved towards him.

Soon, the captains understood that he was not Ahab but they couldn't find him anywhere. Meanwhile, a Syrian soldier's arrow struck King Ahab between the joints of his armour, wounding him. Ahab told his chariot driver to drive off the battlefield. By evening Ahab died his blood stained the chariot. Ahab's body was brought to Samaria. When they washed Ahab's chariot the dogs licked Ahab's blood, just as Elijah had said.

16 The Chariots of Fire

Elijah became old. Elisha, Elijah's son, loved him and was sad that God would soon take him. God told Elijah to visit Bethel. Elisha went too and the prophets told him of Elijah's departure. Elisha went to Jericho and Jordon with Elijah.

Elijah struck the River Jordan with his cloak. It parted and they crossed over. Elijah said, "Elisha, ask anything you want, before I go up."

Elisha said, "Give me a double portion of your spirit!"

Elijah said, "You have asked a hard thing! Only if you see me as I am taken up will you receive this."

Suddenly, a chariot of fire drawn by horses of fire, swept down from Heaven. Elijah went up in a whirlwind! "My father!" cried Elisha. He picked the cloak Elijah had dropped and sadly returned. He struck Jordan with Elijah's robe and it parted. The prophets understood that Elijah's power rested upon Elisha.

17 Elisha Divides the Jordan

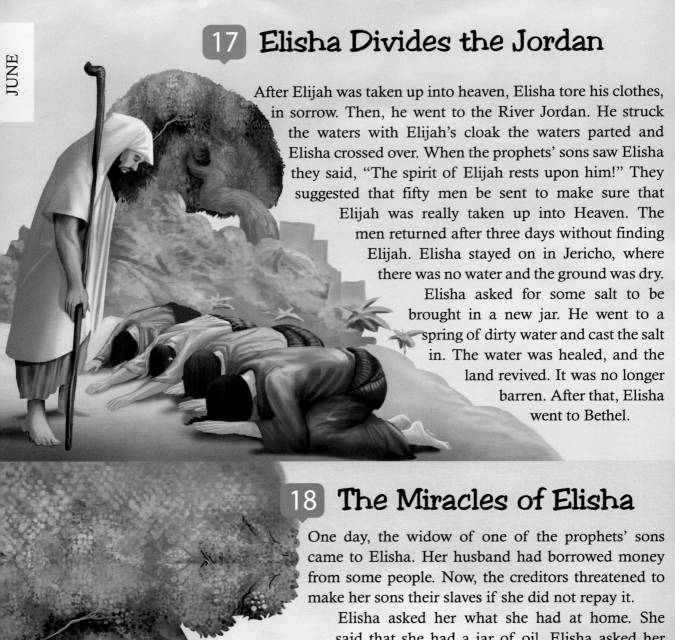

After Elijah was taken up into heaven, Elisha tore his clothes, in sorrow. Then, he went to the River Jordan. He struck the waters with Elijah's cloak the waters parted and Elisha crossed over. When the prophets' sons saw Elisha they said, "The spirit of Elijah rests upon him!" They suggested that fifty men be sent to make sure that Elijah was really taken up into Heaven. The men returned after three days without finding Elijah. Elisha stayed on in Jericho, where there was no water and the ground was dry. Elisha asked for some salt to be brought in a new jar. He went to a spring of dirty water and cast the salt in. The water was healed, and the land revived. It was no longer barren. After that, Elisha went to Bethel.

18 The Miracles of Elisha

One day, the widow of one of the prophets' sons came to Elisha. Her husband had borrowed money from some people. Now, the creditors threatened to make her sons their slaves if she did not repay it.

Elisha asked her what she had at home. She said that she had a jar of oil. Elisha asked her to trust the Lord and borrow vessels from her neighbours. Then, she and her sons were to shut the door. She should pour the oil from her jar into the borrowed vessels until they were filled to the brim. When she obeyed, she found that the oil kept flowing from her jar and the vessels were all full.

She told Elisha what had happened. "Go! Sell the oil and repay the creditors."

She returned, pleased with God's miracle.

19 Elisha and the Kind Lady from Shunem

Whenever Elisha passed through Shunem, he would always be invited for a meal by Shunammite lady. One day, she told her husband, "Elisha is a holy man of God. He often travels through Shunem. Let us build a small room for him. I will put a bed, table, stool and candle stand, so whenever he comes he can have a room to rest."

One day, Elisha and his servant Gehazi arrived and were pleased to stay in the new room. Elisha asked the woman, "What can I do for you, in return for your care?" She did not ask for anything. Then, Gehazi suggested that since the Shunammite had no children, she would be happy to have a baby. Elisha blessed her saying that she would soon have a son. Just as Elisha had said, she had a son.

20 Elisha and the Shunammite's Son

The Shunammite's son soon grew up. One day, he suddenly cried out, "My head!" The Shunammite lady put him on her lap until noon, when he died. Sadly, she placed him on a bed and went to Elisha. When she saw him, she fell on his feet.

"I never asked you for a son," she said, "but you blessed me and now he is dead!"

Elisha sent Gehazi ahead to lay his staff upon the boy. Elisha and the Shunammite followed, but nothing happened. Elisha went into the room. He lay down upon the child, mouth to mouth, eye to eye and hand to hand. The child's body became warm. Elisha walked up and down. He stretched himself out again on the child. The boy sneezed seven times and got up!

107

21 Elisha and the Syrian General

Namaan, a mighty commander in the Syrian army, suffered from leprosy. The Syrians defeated the Israelites. Among the slaves was an Israelite girl, who became Namaan's wife's maidservant. She told Namaan's wife to visit Elisha. Namaan asked the King of Syria, who wrote to the king of Israel, asking for help.

Elisha called Namaan. So, Namaan arrived at his house. Elisha sent a messenger telling Namaan to bathe seven times in the Jordan to be cured. Namaan felt insulted, "Are not the rivers in my country better than the Jordan?"

Still Namaan obeyed Elisha and bathed in the Jordan seven times. Just as Elisha said, Namaan's leprosy disappeared! Namaan said to Elisha, "There is no God in all the Earth like Israel's God."

22 Elisha and the Axe Head

One day, the sons of the prophets asked Elisha, "Let us go to Jordan and make a bigger place to live. Please come with us!" So, Elisha went with them. When they reached Jordan, they began to chop down the trees to clear some place to build their new home.

Suddenly, a man's axe head fell right into the water! "Oh master! What shall I do?" he cried to Elisha, "It was not my axe! I had borrowed it. Please help me!" Elisha asked him to point to the place where the axe head had fallen. Then Elisha cut down a stick and threw it into the water right there. At once, the iron axe head floated and moved towards them! Elisha told the man, "Reach out and take it!" Everyone was amazed at the God's power working through Elisha, which made even an iron axe head float in water!

23 Seeing Eyes Made Blind

The Syrians attacked Israel but Elisha told the King of Israel about all the Syrian King's plans. So the Syrian King thought that someone in his army was revealing all his secrets!

A Syrian soldier said, "Elisha, the prophet, knows what you speak! He tells the King of Israel everything."

The Syrian King wanted to meet Elisha. One morning, Elisha's servant told him that Syrian horses and chariots surrounded the city.

"Don't fear," said Elisha, "We have more on our side than they!"

Then, God showed the servant the mountain full of fiery horses and chariots surrounding Elisha. He went to the Syrian army, "Please make them blind, Lord!" he prayed. Elisha led the blind army to Samaria!

In Samaria, Elisha asked God to return their sight. The Syrian army was very confused. They returned and never troubled Israel again.

24 Hunger Strikes

Ben-hadad, the King of Syria surrounded Samaria with a huge army. There was no food at all. One day, as the King of Israel was walking, a woman told him that because there was no food, another woman told her to kill her son so they could eat him!

Horrified, the king tore his clothes and wore sackcloth of mourning. The king wanted to kill Elisha because he was not helping them. Elisha was in his house with the city elders.

The king's messenger arrived and Elisha told them that God had sent this evil. But, by the next day, Elisha promised there would be lots of food available at very cheap prices. But one of the king's men did not believe it. Elisha said that he would not live to enjoy the food!

25 Lepers Bring Good News

Four lepers lived outside the gates of Samaria, according to Jewish law. One evening, they entered the Syrian camp. To their surprise it was empty! The lepers did not know that God had caused the Syrian army to hear the sound of chariots and horses of a large army coming towards them. They thought that the King of Israel had hired armies to fight them. They left everything and ran for their lives!

The lepers entered the tents, taking food, clothes, gold and silver. Then, a leper said, "Today is a day of good news! Let us go and tell the king now!" The king did not believe them and sent his army after the Syrians. He saw that they had actually fled! Plenty of food at low prices was available. But the man who disbelieved Elisha was trampled to death just as Elisha had said.

26 Isaiah's Vision

When King Uzziah ruled Israel, God gave Isaiah a vision. God sat upon a throne surrounded by Angels, with six wings. They covered their faces and feet with two wings each, with the last pair they flew. They sang, "Holy, holy, holy is the Lord of Hosts; the whole Earth is full of your glory."

The temple doorposts moved and smoke filled the place. Afraid, Isaiah cried, "My lips are sinful. My people, too, are just the same!" An Angel placed a burning piece of coal on Isaiah's mouth, saying, "Your sin is taken away!"

God said, "Who will go for Us and tell the people My message?" Isaiah answered, "Here I am! Send me." God said that Israel would hear His message but not understand it. They would see, but not follow God's laws. He would destroy Israel for their evil ways. Only one-tenth of the people would return to Israel.

27 Isaiah Saves Jerusalem

The people of Judah and Israel went away from God and broke His laws. So, God withheld His help. The Assyrian army conquered one country after another. The King of Judah, Hezekiah, made a treaty with the King of Assyria. He gave away the gold from even the doors of the Lord's temple.

When the Assyrian army still surrounded the city, King Hezekiah sent a messenger to ask Prophet Isaiah for advice. Isaiah assured him that God had promised that the city would not fall to the Assyrians.

King Hezekiah was worried, so he prayed to God. Just as he finished praying, a messenger from Isaiah said, "Do not worry, King, God has heard you! God will defend the city." That very night, the Angel of the Lord destroyed the Assyrian soldiers. Sennacherib, the Assyrian King, returned to Nineveh.

28 Isaiah's Warning to Hezekiah

Once, Hezekiah became very ill. Isaiah, the prophet, told him to set his house in order because God had said he would die. But Hezekiah prayed to God and God healed him and added 15 years to his life. The news of his miraculous recovery reached many places. The ambassador of Babylon came to see him with gifts. This pleased King Hezekiah. From the treasury to the storehouses, the king showed him everything. When Isaiah met Hezekiah, the king told Isaiah everything he had told the ambassador and shown him.

Isaiah told him that the Lord had said, "There will be a day when everything from your palace will be taken to Babylon. Even your very own sons will not be spared!" But Hezekiah was not worried as it did not concern him. He wanted to enjoy peace in his lifetime. He did not worry about what would happen later.

29 Josiah and the Discovery in the Temple

Josiah was only eight years old when he became king. He wanted to bring his people back to God. When Josiah became eighteen, he commanded that the people contribute towards the repair of the temple of Jerusalem. He also held the Passover. While cleaning up, one of his advisors found a the Book of the Law.

When Josiah heard what was written in it, he was very upset. He knew, at once, just how far away from God his people had gone. Then, Josiah read out God's Law in the house of the Lord. He promised, "From this day, we promise to abide by Law and walk after it."

Then, Josiah destroyed all the altars and shrines of Baal.

30 Jeremiah at the Potter's Workshop

God chose many people to be his messengers. These people were simple and God fearing. They had to face many difficulties. But God always gave them strength.

When God chose Jeremiah, he said, "My Lord, I do not know how to speak Your words."

God sent Jeremiah to the potter's house. The potter was making a clay pot, but the pot lost its shape. The potter pressed it again and remade it. God explained, "Jeremiah, My people are like the clay. If they go astray, I will destroy them. If they follow My Commandments, they will be strong. I have chosen you, you have nothing to fear. I will always be with you!"

Jeremiah went to Israel with courage.

01 Jeremiah in Prison

God chose Jeremiah to be his messenger. Jeremiah went to Israel and warned the people. No one believed him and soon, the Babylonians were came to invade them. Jeremiah told them to leave the country, but they stayed and rebelled. More disaster came, each time they ignored his warnings. The leaders said to the king, "Jeremiah is a traitor! You must get rid of him!" The cowardly king said, "Do whatever you want."

"Jeremiah is a man of God. We cannot kill him!" they discussed. Finally, they put him in a deep pit to starve to death. A royal servant, Ebed-melech, an Ethiopian, pleaded for Jeremiah's rescue before the king. The king agreed. Ebed-melech rescued Jeremiah by dropping rags and a rope. Jeremiah put the rags under his arms so that the ropes would not cut into him. Finally, they pulled him out. Jeremiah escaped yet no one listened to him.

02 Daniel and the Special Training

Nebuchadnezzar, the King of Babylon, conquered Israel and took the young and strong as captives. He wanted them to learn the Chaldean culture. Daniel and his friends, Shadrach, Meshach and Abednego were chosen for special training. They were given special food and drink for three years of study.

Daniel decided not to eat the king's food or drink wine. So, he begged the manager to let him eat simple vegetarian food! The manager said that if they looked weak, eating simple food, the king would be angry. But, Daniel wanted to try for ten days. After ten days of simple food, Daniel and his friends looked better than those who ate the king's food! God blessed these four young men with great wisdom and used them in this alien land for His glory.

03 The King's Forgotten Dream

King Nebuchadnezzar told some wise men about a strange dream, which he had forgotten. The wise men were shocked. "Please tell us your dream we will tell you the meaning."

Angry, Nebuchadnezzar ordered them to be killed! Daniel and his friends prayed that God would reveal the dream to them. God showed Daniel the king's dream. Daniel told the king, "No man can tell you your dream. But there is a God in Heaven who reveals secrets. He has shown me your dream."

He said he had seen a huge and bright statue, with a gold head, silver chest and arms, brass stomach and thighs, iron legs and feet of iron and clay. Then, a stone that was not cut by human hands smashed the image. Everything flew like dust in the wind!

115

04 What Does This Dream Mean?

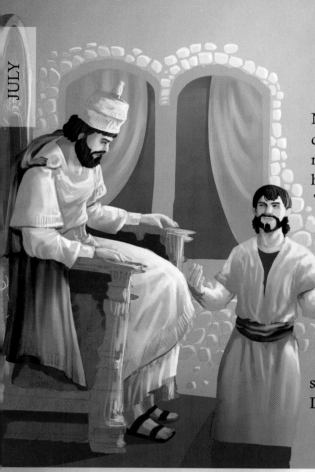

Nebuchadnezzar waited for the explanation of the dream. Daniel told the king, "God has made you a mighty and great king," he said, "You are the gold head! After you, two inferior kingdoms will arise. These are the silver and brass parts of the statue. Finally, a fourth kingdom will arise as strong as iron. But it shall be broken, part iron and part clay! Some parts of the kingdom will be strong and some weak. The stone that could not be cut by human hands is the Kingdom that God Himself shall raise, which can never be destroyed. God wanted you to know this!"

King Nebuchadnezzar fell before Daniel. He said, "Truly your God is God of all Gods!" He gave Daniel a great position in the Kingdom and gifts!

05 Nebuchadnezzar's Own Giant Statue

Once, King Nebuchadnezzar built a tall golden image of himself.

He summoned everyone for the dedication of the image. They were commanded to worship the image at the sound of the music; whoever did not would be thrown into a blazing furnace! As soon as the sound of music was heard, everyone bowed down and worshiped the image. Some astrologers reported to the king, "There are three Jews, Shadrach, Meshach and Abed-nego, who neither worship your gods nor your golden image." The angry king warned the Jews that they would be very severely punished.

They replied, "The God we serve will rescue us from your hand." Furious, Nebuchadnezzar ordered that the furnace be heated seven times hotter to throw the three men in!

06 Four Men in the Furnace

The furnace was heated seven times more. The mightiest men in Nebuchadnezzar's army bound Shadrach, Meshach and Abed-nego, wearing their coats and other clothes, and threw them into the furnace. The men who stood outside the furnace died! To everyone's surprise, four men were seen walking in the furnace instead of three. The fourth looked like the Son of God. Nebuchadnezzar called, "Shadrach, Meshach, Abed-nego, servants of the Most High God, come here!" They walked out of the furnace! The fire had not harmed them.

The king praised the God whom they trusted. He passed a law that anyone speaking anything against the God of Shadrach, Meshach and Abed-nego would be cut into pieces.

07 The Mysterious Handwriting

Once, in a party, King Belshazzar drank wine from gold and silver goblets, which his father took from the temple in Jerusalem and praised other gods. Suddenly, the fingers of a human hand appeared and wrote on the palace wall. The scared king offered a reward to anyone who could read it as none of the wise men in Babylon could. The queen told the king that Daniel.

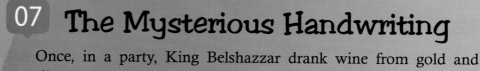

The words written were: 'MENE, MENE, TEKEL, UPHARSIN'. The words meant that God had numbered the days of Belshazzar's reign and brought it to an end. He had been weighed in the scales and found lacking.

His kingdom was divided and given to the Medes and Persians. Daniel was duly rewarded. That very night, King Belshazzar was killed. His kingdom was taken.

08 Plotting Against Daniel

During the reign of King Darius, Daniel was appointed as Chief Administrator to supervise his entire kingdom. The other administrators were unable to find fault with Daniel. They knew they could accuse him only in his personal time with God. So, they requested the king to pass a decree for thirty days, saying that no one should worship any God or man except King Darius!

Anyone disobeying this order would be thrown into the lions' den. Although Daniel knew about the law, he knelt beside the window that faced Jerusalem and prayed three times a day. The others reported Daniel's disobedience to the king. The king was very unhappy to have passed such a law. He really wanted to save Daniel. He told Daniel, "Your God whom you serve continually will save you!" But he could not change his own law, so he finally ordered Daniel to be thrown into the lions' den.

09 Daniel in the Lion's Pit

That night, the king could not sleep or eat. At the break of dawn, he rushed to the lions' den and called out sorrowfully to Daniel. "Daniel! Servant of the living God, did the God you serve continually save you from the lions' mouths?"

Daniel replied, "My God had sent His Angel and shut the mouths of the lions. They have not hurt me at all. I have been innocent of any evil against you or my God." The king was very happy and ordered Daniel to be freed.

He commanded that the false accusers, their wives and children be thrown into the same den. The hungry lions rushed at them and tore them apart and broke their bones! Then, King Darius passed another order that everyone in his kingdom should fear the God of Daniel. If they did not they would be utterly destroyed. So, Daniel prospered well.

10 Ezekiel and the Dry Bones

Once, Prophet Ezekiel had a dream in which the Lord led him to the middle of a valley, full of dry bones. The Lord asked him if these bones could live.

Ezekiel replied, "Dear Lord, you alone know." The Lord asked him to speak to the dry bones, "The Lord says, 'I will make breath come into you and you will come to life. I will attach tendons to you and make flesh come upon you and cover you with skin; I will put breath in you, and you will come to life. Then you will know that I am the Lord.'"

The Lord asked him to command breath over them. Breath entered and a big army stood before him. The Lord explained that the dry bones were the people of Israel without hope. Ezekiel should tell them that God would take them to Israel.

11 The Story of the Returning Exiles

Prophet Jeremiah had warned the people of Judah. But they ignored his warnings. Everything happened just as Jeremiah foretold. Often, people would sing songs about Jerusalem. People were losing hope, so God called upon his prophets, Jeremiah and Ezekiel.

"Tell my people not to lose hope. I am still with them. Tell them to settle down in Babylon and live according to my Law. One day, I will restore all their land and happiness." People in Babylon had hope again. "One day, I am going to make a new Covenant with my people, and forgive all their mistakes," the Lord promised.

12 Nehemiah Rebuilds Jerusalem

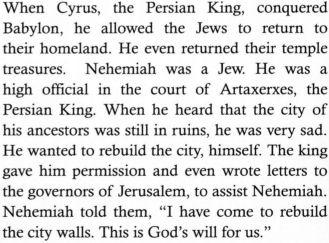

When Cyrus, the Persian King, conquered Babylon, he allowed the Jews to return to their homeland. He even returned their temple treasures. Nehemiah was a Jew. He was a high official in the court of Artaxerxes, the Persian King. When he heard that the city of his ancestors was still in ruins, he was very sad. He wanted to rebuild the city, himself. The king gave him permission and even wrote letters to the governors of Jerusalem, to assist Nehemiah. Nehemiah told them, "I have come to rebuild the city walls. This is God's will for us."

Then, he assigned work to each family. They had to build one part of the walls. Although it seemed impossible, Nehemiah encouraged the people until they finished building the city walls in fifty-two days. Finally, the day arrived to dedicate the walls to the Lord.

13 The Story of Esther

In the third year of his reign, King Xerxes gave a party for all his nobles and officials. Then, he displayed the wealth of his kingdom for 180 days. After that he gave another party for seven days for everyone in Susa.

Queen Vashti had also thrown a party for the ladies. At the end of the seventh day, King Xerxes ordered his beautiful queen to show her beauty to his guests. The queen refused to obey the king's order. This angered the king and he ordered that Vashti to never enter in his presence again.

An order was passed to look for young and beautiful girls for the king. A Jew, Mordecai, adopted his cousin Esther, a beautiful girl. Soon, Esther's turn came to go before the king. The king found her more beautiful than anyone else and made her queen. The king threw a party to celebrate the crowning of Esther.

14 Mordecai and Haman

Kings Xerxes commanded the royal officials to pay respect to Haman. But Mordecai would not bow before Haman. The officials reported Mordecai's behaviour to Haman and that Mordecai was a Jew. Haman thought of a way to kill Mordecai and all Jews. He approached King Xerxes and explained that some people in the kingdom followed different customs. It would not be good for the king to tolerate them. If the king agreed, then a law could be issued to kill all of them.

The king agreed to Haman's suggestion. Then, an order, signed by the king was sent out throughout the kingdom to kill all Jews on a certain date. Mordecai was very sad. He mourned outside the king's gate. He sent a message to Queen Esther explaining the king's order to kill the Jews. He asked her to plead before the king for the lives of her people.

15 A Queenly Request

Anyone who approached the king without being called by him could be put to death. Only the king could spare that person's life by extending his golden sceptre to him. Queen Esther sent a message asking Mordecai to gather all the Jews at Susa. They had to fast and pray for three days. She too would do the same. After that, she would meet the king and plead for the lives of her people.

When Queen Esther went to meet the king, he was pleased. He asked, "Queen Esther, what is your request? I would give you even half of my kingdom." The queen then invited him and Haman for a banquet that day.

At the banquet, the queen invited them to another banquet the next day. The king read in the records in the banquet of how Mordecai had saved his life. He wanted to reward him for his good actions.

16 A Day of Remembrance

The king asked the queen at the banquet what she desired. The queen told him that they had been sold to be slaughtered. She pleaded for her life and the life of her people. The angry king asked, "Where is the man who dared do such a thing?"

The queen replied, "Haman."

Haman pleaded with the queen for his life. The king ordered that Haman be hanged. Esther fell at the king's feet and wept. She pleaded that an order be passed to overrule Haman's wicked plan to destroy the Jews.

The king agreed and with his approval, Mordecai made a decree. The Jews were given the right to protect themselves against anyone who attacked them.

17 Satan Challenges God About Job

Once, Job, a rich and God-fearing man lived in Uz. He had seven sons and three daughters, who often enjoyed times together. After every celebration, Job would pray for his children. One day, the Angels presented themselves before God and the devil came, too. The Lord asked Satan, "Where have you come from?" He replied, "From Earth."

The Lord asked him if he had seen anyone else like Job, who feared God and hated evil. Satan challenged God by saying that Job feared Him only because He had blessed the work of Job's hand and protected him. Satan said, "God, if You take away what Job has, he will curse You to Your face!" The Lord told Satan, "All that Job owns is in your hands. You test him. Only do not touch him." Satan left to test Job.

18 Job's Troubles

One day, Job's children had a party in their oldest brother's house. Many messengers came to Job with sad news, the Sabeans had destroyed the cattle and servants. A fire from heaven burnt the sheep and shepherds and the Chaldeans stole all the camels! All his children had died in a terrible windstorm.

Job tore his clothes and shaved his head. He said he was born in this world without anything and he would die exactly like that! He never blamed God for anything. Satan approached God and said, "If Job's body were struck, he would surely curse You."

The Lord told Satan to touch Job's body with illness, but not to kill him. Satan sent sores all over Job's body. Sitting among ashes, Job scraped his sores with a piece of pottery. His wife saw his suffering, "Curse God and die!" she advised. Job only scolded her for her foolishness.

19 Job's Friends

Job's three friends heard about his troubles. They came to comfort him. When they saw Job they could not recognise him. They cried aloud, tore their clothes and sat on the ground with him. They did not speak a word for seven days and nights. Job spoke up at last. He said he was sad because although he trusted God he did not understand why such troubles had befallen him.

His friends told Job he must have done something really wicked. They also condemned God. But Job did not agree with his friends and said, "No, I have not sinned. I have lived a good life. I have worshiped God. I have been kind to the poor. The things you say about God and me are not true."

20 God Answers Job

Suddenly, God spoke out of a whirlwind. He told Job that he would ask questions and Job would answer them. He reminded them that He was the Almighty Creator of the Earth and everything in it. After Job heard God's voice, he realised how holy and wonderful God was and that he was actually a sinner. Job told God, "I have heard You in my ears, but now I have seen You and I hate myself. I know that I am a sinner. I am sorry."

Job knew that he was not good in God's sight and God had a right to do with him just as He wished. God told Job's friends that they had sinned in talking as they did. They should offer a sacrifice and ask Job to pray for them. Job prayed for his friends, and then they offered a sacrifice as instructed. Job was healed of the boils.

21 Israel's Hymn Book

The Psalms are a very special part of the Old Testament in the Bible. The word 'Psalm' means song. This book is a collection of 150 songs and poems meant to be sung with musical instruments.

The Psalms are broadly divided into five sections. There are some very well-known Psalms like Psalm 1, which teaches us that we must love God. Psalm 2 tells us that God will rule the world. Psalm 23 tells of how God as a Shepherd loves His sheep. In Psalm 51, David confesses his sin. The longest Psalm is 119 with 176 verses. The shortest is Psalm 117 with only two verses.

Many people wrote the Psalms, but King David was known to be the foremost contributor of Psalms.

22 Proverbs of Solomon

King Solomon, son of King David, was known for his wisdom and he wrote the Book of Proverbs. He explained the difference between wise and foolish behaviour. The book says, "The wise store up knowledge, but the mouth of a fool invites ruin."

It says, "The fear of the Lord is the beginning of wisdom." It also tells that the way of the world is not always the way of God. It can lead to death.

The promise given in this book is that those who choose wisdom and follow God will be blessed in many ways. But those who reject Him will surely suffer shame and death.

23 Hosea

Hosea was a man from the northern kingdom of Israel. He had married a woman called Gomer. Hosea liked a quiet life but Gomer enjoyed time with other men. They had three children. But, one day, Gomer left home and never returned.

Hosea was very sad. He really loved his wife and kept searching for her. When he finally found her, he begged her to return. Gomer returned but she left him again and again.

Hosea gave up trying to get his wife back. He had to bring up his children and they left him when they grew up. This experience taught him a great deal about God. He learnt that Israel was God's wife. Just like Gomer, Israel would be unfaithful to God again and again. Though God might punish her, He would always bring her back into His loving arms.

24 Amos, the Shepherd

Amos was a simple and kind shepherd. He loved God and lived by his Commandments. One day, he went to the prosperous town of Bethel. He was saddened to see the idolatry there. The merchants had earned their riches through wrong means.

The courts did not give proper justice. They were partial towards the rich. Even the priests had no sympathy for the people's problems.

Seeing this, Amos proclaimed to the people of Bethel, "Prepare to meet your God! You all have become slaves of the evil ways, you must seek God. Otherwise you will be punished! God will send severe famine and many will be destroyed. But there is still hope. God will not forget his chosen people. He will give them prosperity, once they repent of their evil ways and return to Him."

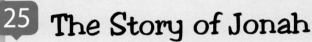

25 The Story of Jonah

Nineveh was one of the greatest cities, although its residents were very evil. God told Jonah to warn the people of Nineveh that if they did not change their wicked ways, He would destroy them in forty days.

But Jonah did not listen to god and took a ship sailing to the opposite direction from Nineveh. God sent a big storm and the ship got caught in it. The sailors threw many things from the ship to keep it from sinking.

Jonah was sleeping. The captain woke him up, "How can you sleep? Get up and pray!" The sailors wanted to know the cause of God's wrath and Prophet Jonah had to confess that he had disobeyed God. He told them to throw him into the sea. When they did, the winds stopped and the sea became calm. All the sailors worshipped and offered sacrifices to God in fear.

26 Jonah and Castor Oil Plant

God sent a big fish to swallow Jonah. For three days and three nights, Jonah stayed in the belly of the fish, praying. He was sorry and called on God for help. God instructed the fish to vomit Jonah on dry land.

Jonah heard God again. He went to Nineveh and preached to the people. Jonah said, "Forty more days and God will overthrow Nineveh!" The people of Nineveh heard Jonah and believed God. They repented from their wicked ways. The king heard what Jonah said and he too took off his royal robe and sat on the dust, fasting and praying.

The king passed a decree: people of Nineveh would not eat or drink anything and will be covered with sackcloth. He hoped God would have compassion and not destroy them. God heard their prayers and saw that they had truly changed from their evil ways. He did not destroy them.

27 Lessons from the Small Worm

The Lord spared the people in Nineveh. Jonah, angrily, told the Lord that this was why he had run away earlier to Tarshish. He said, "I know you are gracious and loving. You change your mind and don't destroy. Yet these people were cruel to us."

The Lord said that He had not given up on Jonah when he disobeyed Him. He forgave Jonah when he repented. While Jonah sat outside the city, the Lord made a vine grow, which gave shade. Jonah was comfortable.

Next morning, the Lord sent a worm, which chewed up the vine. Jonah felt bad. The Lord said, "You were concerned about an ordinary vine, which grew on its own and withered. Nineveh has many people whom I made. Are they not more valuable to me than the vine?"

28 Micah's Prophecy

The people of Micah's town slowly grew away from God. Micah loved God and could not bear to see this. When harvest failed, farmers borrowed from moneylenders. If they were unable to pay back, the moneylenders seized their lands and sold them as slaves! Even the priests were not honest before God. Micah warned the people, saying, "God doesn't like your evil ways; you will be punished severely!"

The people did not listen to his warning. They thought God would protect them. Micah told them, "God will leave the holy temple if you continue. Jerusalem will be ploughed like a field and the place where the temple stands would be ruined! But the future is hopeful. A special person would come, a Man from Bethlehem to rule Israel. He will be God's own Messenger, His Glory and His Majesty—the Lord Jesus!"

29 God's Promise to Save Jerusalem

Zechariah was a prophet during the reign of King Darius. God gave him visions about the time Lord Jesus would come as Saviour. Once, Zechariah saw a vision of an Angel carrying a measuring scale to measure the length and breadth of Jerusalem.

Another Angel came and told the first Angel to tell Zechariah that Jerusalem would be so full of people and cattle that it would be like a town without walls. The Lord, Himself would be as a wall of fire, protecting Jerusalem and He, Himself, would be the glory within the city. God says He would care for Jerusalem, so tenderly that anyone touching Jerusalem would actually be touching the very apple of His eye! He would destroy anyone who attacked Jerusalem. They would then know that God, Himself protects Jerusalem.

Many other nations would come to Jerusalem and become God's own people. This will happen when the Messiah or 'Anointed One' would come.

30 Vision about the High Priest

Zechariah saw another vision, this time about Joshua, the High Priest. He saw Joshua standing before God. Satan stood at Joshua's right. God scolds Satan, saying that He has chosen Jerusalem as His holy city and Joshua is like a brand saved from the fire.

Joshua is wearing dirty clothes. "I have taken away your sin and will give you a change of clothes," said God in the vision. A beautiful mitre or special cap was put on his head. Now, Joshua stood clean and dressed in fresh clothes, like a priest.

The Angel warned Joshua, "If you keep God's Commandments and walk in His ways, you shall judge my people. I will lead you in places among those that stand by." God promised to send Lord Jesus to deliver all mankind from sin. A name God used for Him is 'the Branch' and He will remove all sin when He comes.

Malachi—My Messenger Will Come

The name Malachi means 'His Messenger'. The message in this book is for the Israelites. The message is that the great king is coming. Although the Jews had returned to their own land from exile and rebuilt the temple, they were very discouraged. Their land lay just behind the mighty Persian kingdom. The glorious future, which the prophets had foretold, had not yet happened. God had not come to inhabit the temple. So, they doubted God's love and lost hope.

Malachi told the people not to doubt God's love. He announced with a warning that God was coming to judge like a 'refiner's fire'; but He would first judge His own people.

God does not change in His commitment. Therefore, Israel had not been completely destroyed for her persistent unfaithfulness. Only if they repented they could experience His blessing again. Those who honour God will be spared when He comes to judge.

THE
NEW

TESTAMENT

01 The Old and the New Testament

The word 'Covenant' means Promise. The Bible is divided into the Old Covenant or Old Testament and the New Covenant or New Testament. The Old Covenant was God's promise to Israel, His chosen people. He brought them out of slavery and idolatry and established them as a nation, fighting their wars, healing their illnesses and giving them His laws to follow. He punished them when they turned away from Him. Finally, through the prophets, He promised to send a Saviour to save them from their sins.

According to the Old Covenant, a sinful man could reach God only by offering sacrifices for his sin. As per the New Covenant, the crucifixion of the Lord Jesus is the ultimate sacrifice for the sins of the whole world. No more sacrifice is required. His believers and followers do not fear death because of His resurrection. Instead, they hope that He will return to take them to Heaven to live with them forever.

02 The New Covenant

The New Covenant is the story of the Lord Jesus, God's own Son. He was a God as well as a Man. He brought God and Man into a close relationship by his death on the cross.

The New Covenant is a collection of over twenty books. Lord Jesus lived in the land of Palestine about two thousand years ago and the books were written by his followers. The language used for writing at that time was Greek. Fragments of very early written pages still exist.

The first four of the books of the New Testament are called the Gospels and they are four accounts of the life of Jesus, as told by Matthew, Mark, Luke and John. After the Gospels comes the book of Acts, which is an account of what happened to his followers next. Most of the other books are letters written by leading Christians.

03 The Coming of the Romans

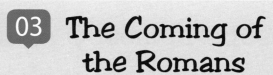

The Prophets had foretold that the Messiah would come to save Israel. However, four hundred years passed by and God's Anointed One still had not come. The Israelites fought many wars. Their land was taken away by the Greek kings. Then, a hero, Judas Maccabeus, defeated the Greeks. However, the Romans invaded Palestine. The Roman army was strong and defeated the Greeks.

Herod, a cruel king, ruled Palestine during the time of Christ. He ordered his soldiers and officials to collect tax money. Everyone disliked him. The Jewish people dreamt of the day when a new king would come to save them from the Roman kings. The Romans did not worship the God of Israel. Caesar was their God! That is why Herod was so amazed at Lord Jesus's claim to be the Son of God and the King of the Jews!

04 A Baby for Elizabeth

In the 400 year gap between the events in Old and New Testament, King David's empire fought a series of war with the Macedonians and lost. Later the Mocedonians were defeated by the Romans. Thus in the beginning of New Testament, the Romans were in power. During the rule of King Herod, there was a priest named Zacharias who obeyed all the commandments.

One day, Angel Gabriel appeared before Zacharias while he was praying. Angel Gabriel said, "Your prayer has been answered. Your wife, Elizabeth, will bear you a baby boy. You are to name him, John, who would grow up and prepare the people for the coming of the Saviour."

Zacharias asked, "How is that possible?" Gabriel was angry and said, "Because you did not believe the word of God, you shall not be able to speak till the day the baby is born."

05 Mary is Chosen

Among the hills of Galilee, there was a town called Nazareth. A girl called Mary lived there, who was a descendent of King David and a cousin of Zacharias's wife Elizabeth. When she reached a marriageable age, her family arranged for her to marry Joseph.

One day, God sent Angel Gabriel to give Mary an important message. When Mary was busy with her household chores, the Angel Gabriel greeted her, "Peace be with you! The Lord has greatly blessed you."

Mary was deeply troubled by the angel's message and wondered what his words meant.

06 The Story of the Birth of Jesus

When Angel Gabriel visited Mary again and said, "Don't be afraid, Mary; God has been gracious to you. You will bear a son, the Son of High God. You shall name him Jesus and God will make him a king of descendants of David."

Mary asked the angel, "How is that possible? I am a virgin and have no husband."

Then, Angel Gabriel explained to Mary, "The Holy Spirit will come on you and God's power will rest upon you. For this reason the holy child will be called the Son of God. Remember your relative Elizabeth? It was said that she can never carry a child, yet she is carrying a child in her old age."

Mary said, "I am the Lord's servant." The angel left her. As Mary was a servant of God, she accepted what the Angel had told her.

07 Mary Visits Elizabeth

Soon, Mary went to Judah to meet Elizabeth. When Elizabeth heard Mary's greetings, the baby in Elizabeth's womb moved. The Holy Spirit came upon Elizabeth and spoke in a loud voice, "You are blessed among all women and blessed is the child that will be born to you. Why would such a great thing happen to me that the mother of my Lord has come to meet me? As soon as I heard your voice, the baby inside me jumped with joy. How happy you are to believe that God's promise to you will come true."

Happily, Mary sang a song and praised God for having chosen her among all the women. Mary happily stayed with Elizabeth for three months and then returned home to Nazareth.

08 The Birth of John, the Baptist

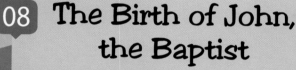

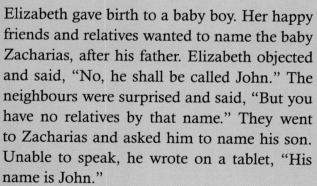

Elizabeth gave birth to a baby boy. Her happy friends and relatives wanted to name the baby Zacharias, after his father. Elizabeth objected and said, "No, he shall be called John." The neighbours were surprised and said, "But you have no relatives by that name." They went to Zacharias and asked him to name his son. Unable to speak, he wrote on a tablet, "His name is John."

That very moment, the curse was lifted and Zacharias was able to speak again. All the neighbours were surprised. They wondered, "What is this child going to be?" For it was plain that the Lord's power was upon him.

Zacharias praised God and foretold that John would be a saviour. He would go before the Lord and prepare the way for His coming.

09 Mary, Joseph and the Dream

Mary was now engaged to Joseph, a young carpenter. He learned that Mary was going to be the mother. He was a good man and he did not want Mary to face any shame, but could not come to terms with it. He did not know that the baby in Mary's womb was the son of the Lord.

One night, an angel visited Joseph in his dream. He told Joseph, "Don't be afraid. You must marry Mary because she carries the son of the Lord in her womb, conceived when the Holy Spirit came upon her. The child should be named 'Jesus'. He will save people from their sins."

Joseph did just as the angel had said. He married Mary and took care of her.

10 Baby Jesus

During the rule of King Herod, an order was passed. Everybody had to return to their home town and register themselves with the authorities. They wanted to count the number of people in every town in order to tax them.

So, Joseph and Mary left the town of Nazareth and went to the town of Bethlehem, the birth place of King David.

The inn at Bethlehem had no room for them. The innkeeper offered them his stable where he kept his animals.

Mary gave birth to a baby boy in the stable. The baby was laid in a manger as there was no crib. Mary named him Jesus. The Saviour Lord had arrived.

11 The Shepherds and the Angels

In the fields near Bethlehem, some shepherds were watching sheep. When Lord Jesus was born, an angel appeared to them.

The shepherds were afraid. The angel said, "Do not be afraid, I have good news for you. Today, in David's town, a Saviour is born. He is Jesus Christ, the Lord. You will find him lying in a manger in a stable."

More angels appeared and praised God. One of the shepherds said, "Let us go to Bethlehem, and see the baby the angel told us about." They found Mary and Joseph along with the baby in a manger. They were overjoyed to see Jesus and went away singing praises to the Lord. They told the news of the birth of the Saviour to everyone they met.

12 The Wise Men Find Jesus

Herod was a very wicked king. He sent three wise men to Bethlehem, saying, "Go and search for the child, the Saviour who will take birth soon. Once you have found him, let me know so that I can also go and worship him."

The wise men travelled, till they reached Bethlehem the night Jesus was born. A star shone brightly in the sky. The three wise men decided to follow the star which led them to the stable Jesus was in. They went inside and found Him. They worshipped the child and gave him the precious gifts. The wise men left the stable and started their journey back to King Herod's palace. As they slept at night, an angel visited them in their dream and warned them not to return to Herod. So, they decided to return to their home without ever telling Herod about baby Jesus.

13 The Escape to Egypt

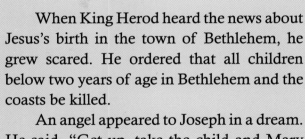

When King Herod heard the news about Jesus's birth in the town of Bethlehem, he grew scared. He ordered that all children below two years of age in Bethlehem and the coasts be killed.

An angel appeared to Joseph in a dream. He said, "Get up, take the child and Mary and escape to Egypt. Stay there till I tell you. King Herod is searching for the child and wants to kill him."

Joseph obeyed and left for Egypt. They stayed there till King Herod died. Finally, the angel told Joseph that it was safe to return to Israel but when Joseph heard that Herod's son, Archelaus was the next king, he was afraid that he, too, would want to kill Jesus. So, Joseph settled in Nazareth. Jesus grew up in Nazareth and was called a Nazarene.

14 The Story of Boy Jesus

Every year, Mary, Joseph and Jesus went to Jerusalem for the Feast of Passover. Once when Jesus was twelve years old, Joseph and Mary returned to Nazareth only to realise that Jesus was not with them.

They looked for him everywhere but were unable to find him. When they returned to Jerusalem after three days, they saw him sitting in the temple talking to the teachers. His parents were surprised to see Him talking to learned teachers. Then, His mother asked Him why He had stayed back. Jesus replied, "Why were you searching for me? Did you not know I would be in my Father's house? Where else will I be?"

They all returned to Nazareth. Jesus grew up to be very wise.

145

15 The Story of John, the Baptist

John was a very wise and a hard-working person. One day, while he was in the desert, God spoke to him and told him about Jesus, the Saviour who will free people from their sins.

Then, John preached to people preparing them for the coming of the Lord Jesus. He baptised many in the River Jordan.

John told people to change their ways. He said that those who had two sets of clothes were to give away one set to the needy. He also told the tax collectors not to collect extra money. He told the soldiers to avoid violence.

All those who heard John wondered if he was the Saviour. John answered them saying that he only baptised with water and Jesus, who was coming, will baptise them with the Holy Spirit.

16 Jesus is Baptised

When Jesus was about thirty years old, he came to River Jordan. John, the Baptist, was baptising people there.

Jesus asked John to baptise Him too. But John refused as he knew that Jesus was the Son of God, who had been sent to save the world. John asked Jesus why He had come to him to be baptised.

Jesus explained that John had to baptise Him so that he fulfils the word of God. John obeyed Jesus and baptised Him in the river.

Just as, Jesus was baptised, the Heavens opened. The Holy Spirit, in the form of a dove, rested upon Jesus. A voice from Heaven said, "This is my beloved Son who will fulfil my promise to the people."

17 Jesus and Satan

The Holy Spirit that rested upon Jesus after He was baptised led Him to the desert for forty days. Jesus neither ate nor drank anything.

He was hungry. Satan, the devil, wanted to test him and asked Jesus to change the stones into bread if He was truly the Son of God. Jesus replied, "Man shall not live by bread alone, but by every word of God."

Satan led Jesus to a high mountain and told Him that he would give Him power over the world if Jesus would worship him. Jesus replied, "It is written, worship the Lord, your God, and serve Him only." Satan then led Jesus to the highest point of the mountain. He told Lord Jesus to throw Himself down. If he was really the Son of God then surely the angels would hold Him up. Then, Jesus said, "Do not put God to test." Hearing this, Satan left Him.

18 The First Disciples

John the Baptist told the people to repent for their evil ways and turn to God. He preached about the Messiah, whom God had sent to save the people from their sins.

One day, John was standing with his two disciples, when he saw Jesus walking by. John exclaimed, "Look! The Son of God!" John's disciples followed Jesus. He turned to them and asked, "What are you looking for?"

They replied, "Lord, where do you live?" Jesus invited them, "Come and see!" They went with Him. One of the disciples, Andrew, returned home and told his brother, Simon, "We have found the Messiah, the Christ, God's Anointed One, the very One that John, the Baptist told us about!"

Andrew brought Simon to Jesus, who said, "You are Simon, son of Jona. Hereafter, you shall be called Cephas, which means 'Stone'."

19 Jesus Chooses Twelve Disciples

Walking by the Sea of Galilee, Jesus called Simon Peter and his brother, Andrew. They were casting a net into the sea. Jesus said, "Follow me! And from now on you shall catch men." They followed him without asking anything.

Then, Jesus called two other fishermen, James and John, the sons of Zebedee. They left everything and followed Jesus.

The next day, Jesus saw Philip walking on the road and said, "Follow me."

Jesus then called Matthew, the tax collector, to follow him. Then, Jesus chose Thomas, Bartholomew, James, the son of Alphaeus, Thaddeus (also called Judas, brother of James) and Simon, the zealot and Judas Iscariot.

Thus, Jesus chose twelve disciples. They were always with Him, learning from Him and carrying out His wishes. But it was Judas Iscariot, who finally betrayed Jesus.

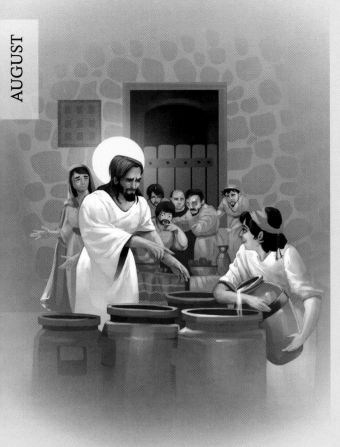

20 The First Miracle

Once, Jesus, His disciples and Mary attended a wedding in Cana in Galilee. Soon, they learnt about the unexpected lack of wine.

Jesus told the servants to fill six stone jars with water. The jars were filled to the brim. Then, He asked the servants to serve the water to the host of the wedding. The host tasted the water and it tasted like wine. The water had turned into wine!

The host said, "This is the best wine I have had till now."

This was the first miracle Jesus performed.

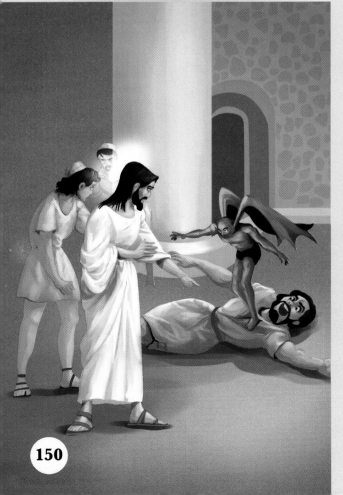

21 Man with the Evil Spirit

Jesus arrived at the town of Capernaum with His disciples. On the day of Sabbath, Jesus went to the Synagogue to teach. The people who heard Him were amazed. They had not heard anyone speak so confidently, with authority and power.

Just then, a crooked recognised Jesus and shouted, "I know you have come to destroy us. I know who you are, the Son of God."

Jesus spoke sternly at him and said, "Be quiet and come out of him." The man shook violently and gave a loud shriek, and an evil spirit left his body. The people who saw this were astonished. News about Jesus and His magical power spread all over Galilee.

22 Jesus Heals Peter's Mother-in-law

One day, Jesus and His disciples, went to Simon Peter's house to see him. Simon Peter informed Him that his mother-in-law was not well. Lord Jesus requested to be taken to see her at once. He went inside the room where she was resting, took her by her hand and lifted her up.

At once, the fever left her body. She got up feeling completely well. Everyone who heard about the miracle was amazed. They had never seen anyone with fever recover so quickly. By evening, the people living nearby brought all those who were ill to Peter's door! It seemed like the entire city was gathered around Peter's house. Jesus healed many people suffering from different kinds of illnesses. He cast out many evil spirits.

23 Jesus Visits Nazareth

Jesus continued doing the work God sent Him for in various towns that he visited. Wherever He went, He taught in the Synagogues and everyone who heard Him was enthralled.

Soon, Jesus visited Nazareth, his hometown. He went to the Synagogue and started to read out from a scroll.

Someone recognised Jesus and whispered, "Isn't this Joseph's son?"

Jesus explained that as the people in the town have seen him grow up, they will find it difficult to believe Him and in His powers.

The people were angry and they chased Him out of town. But, Jesus walked through the middle of the crowd and disappeared.

24 John is Imprisoned

John the Baptist had his own disciples. He became so popular that people wondered if he was the Messiah. But he clearly said that he was not the Son of God, but was sent ahead of Him.

Princess Herodias, King Herod's daughter-in-law, hated John and requested him to throw John in the prison. King Herod knew John was a holy man and liked listening to him, but he gave in to Herodias's request and imrisoned John.

John could not continue his work. John's disciples were disturbed. They asked Jesus whether He was truly the Messiah. Jesus told them to tell John about all the miracles that they saw Jesus do. John was happy when his disciples told him about Jesus's miracles.

25 Reward for a Dance

It was King Herod's birthday and a big banquet was held in his honour.

At the banquet, Princess Herodias's daughter, Salome, danced before the guests. King Herod was so pleased that he promised to give her whatever she requested. She requested for John the Baptist's head on a plate, as her mother hated John and Salome wanted to please her mother.

King Herod was upset, but he had promised to give whatever she asked. He ordered the executioners to behead John. They did so and brought John's head on a platter. Herod presented it to Salome and she gave it to her mother.

26 The Sermon on the Mount

Jesus climbed up a mountainside and taught His disciples about the Beatitudes. He explained how God blesses people depending on their attitudes. The poor who realise they need God are promised that the Kingdom of Heaven belongs to them. God Himself will comfort those who mourn and grieve. The humble and contented ones will own the Earth. Those who are passionate for Godly things will receive deep satisfaction from following them. Care and mercy will be shown to those who are merciful and caring. Those who keep their hearts and minds clean will surely see God. Those who work for peace will find their place in the family of God as His children.

27 The Light of the World

Once, Jesus was explaining to his disciples the importance of salt and light.

He said, "Salt adds flavour to food and light helps us to see."

Jesus told them that they are the salt of the Earth. If the salt loses its flavour, it becomes useless and is fit only to be thrown down and trampled under men's feet! So, the disciples were instructed to be 'the salt' among the people.

He told His disciples that they were the light of the world. A lit lamp should be kept on a stand so that it gives out light to everyone. All that is good and bad can be seen.

Jesus told the disciples to be 'the light' in the world.

28 Jesus Teaches About Prayer

One day, Jesus was teaching His disciples about true prayer. First, He told them how not to pray.

He said, "There are some people who pretend to be good and honourable. These kinds of people like to stand and pray in public places. They do so, as they want everyone to see them and praise them for their faith and dedication. Their faith towards God is superficial. So, people should not stand at public places and pray."

Then Jesus taught His disciples the right way to pray. He told them that they were to close the door of their room. Then, they should pray in private to God. It is then that their prayers would be truly rewarded.

29 The Prayer

Jesus also told the disciples that God, the Father in Heaven, knows what people need even before they ask Him for those things.

Then, Jesus taught them a prayer, which today is commonly called the Lord's Prayer:

"Our Father in Heaven, blessed is Your name. Your kingdom come, Your will be done on Earth as it is in Heaven.

Give us today our daily bread.

Forgive us our sins, as we forgive those who have sinned against us.

Lead us not to temptation.

But deliver us from the evil one.

For Yours is the Kingdom, the power and the glory forever.

Amen."

30 The Two Prayers

Jesus told another parable to some people who always thought they were much better or holier than others. Once, two men went to the temple to pray. One was a teacher of the law and the other was a collector of tax.

The teacher of the law stood up, praying loudly, "Oh, God, I thank you that I am not like other people—dishonest, greedy, unfaithful in marriage and particularly not like this tax collector. I fast twice a week and give tithes on all my income."

The tax collector was sorry for the wrong he had done and prayed, "God, have mercy on me. Forgive me for I am a sinner." Jesus remarked, "The tax collector got right with God before he went home but the teacher of law did not." Jesus explained that anyone who is proud will always be brought down, whereas, God would always lift the humble.

31 A Friend Visits at Midnight

Jesus told a story to show how prayer works, "At midnight, your friend visits you after a long journey and there is no bread to offer him. You go to another friend's house and borrow bread. That friend could say that he is already in bed, and he doesn't want to be disturbed. He may not get up and give you bread because you are his friend but because you are persistent in asking."

Jesus affirmed that if anyone asks, he will surely receive. When anyone seeks he will find what he is looking for and when he knocks, the door will definitely be opened.

Jesus then tells everyone present there, "Our Heavenly Father will certainly give the Holy Spirit to those who ask Him."

01 The Two Builders

Jesus used parables, stories from life on Earth with religious meanings, to teach His disciples.

He said that those who obey His words are wise whereas those who do not put His teachings into practice are foolish. Jesus gave the example of a wise and a foolish man. The wise man is the one who built his house with rocks. One day, it rained and the water rose; the winds blew and beat against the house. But, that house stood firm, as the foundation was solid.

The foolish man built a house of sand. The rains came and water rose; winds blew and beat against the house. That house crashed to the ground. Jesus was comparing the house to people and the storm to the problems of life.

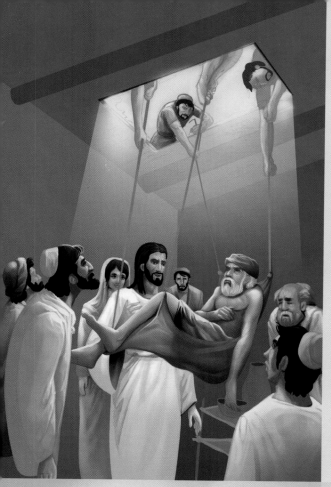

02 Four Friends Make a Way

Once, Jesus was teaching when he saw four men carrying a paralysed man on a mat to the house. They had heard a lot about the miracles performed by Jesus. But, the house was very crowded. As they could not carry him through the door, they climbed up to the roof, took off the tiles. So through the roof they lowered him and laid him before Jesus.

Jesus said, "Son, your sins are forgiven."

The teachers of the law knew only God could forgive sins, and to them Jesus was just another man. Jesus knew their thoughts, He informed them that the Son of God had the right on earth to forgive sins.

Turning to the paralysed man on the mat, he said, "Go home." The man stood up, took his mat and went home, praising the Lord.

03 The Kingdom of Heaven

Once, Jesus was expounding parables about the Kingdom of Heaven to a crowd.

He said, "Once an honest man sowed good seeds in his field. His enemy quietly sowed weeds among the wheat. The wheat and weeds sprouted. The man thought that at harvest, the weeds would be bundled and thrown into the fire and the wheat would be gathered in the barn." When the people looked perplexed, Jesus explained the meaning. He said, "The man who sowed the seeds is the Son of Man. The field is the world. Good seeds are the people and weeds are evil. God will send his angels, the servants, who will weed out the evil. Then, the evil will be thrown into hell and the people will be recieved in the Kingdom of Heaven."

157

04 The Sower

At the Lake of Galilee, a huge crowd gathered to hear Lord Jesus's parables. Jesus got into a boat and said, "Once, a farmer sowed seeds. He scattered some on the roadside and the birds ate them up. Some fell on the rocks and so the plants could not take root. The seeds that fell among thorns got choked. The ones that fell on good soil grew well."

He explained, "The seed represents the Word of God. People who hear the word of God but allow Satan to snatch it away are like the seeds fallen by the roadside. The ones on rocky ground are like people who hear the word but change their minds when troubles come. The thorny ground represents people who hear the word, but allow the worries of the world to make them unfruitful. The good soil signifies people who accept the word and bear good fruit."

05 The Leaven

One day, as Jesus was addressing a gathering, he said, "The Kingdom of Heaven is like a lady making bread at home. When the bread is being made, a little yeast is always added and kneaded well into the dough. After the dough is left for a while in an oven, it starts to rise and becomes double its size!"

He explained, "This is exactly how God's Kingdom grows. You may not be able to see how it happens, but those who believe in God will see their lives changing. God is at work deep within their lives making a definite visible difference. Those who follow me will be different from those who do not, in their very thoughts and actions. God's Kingdom, thus, grows by God's power to transform the believers' lives."

06 The Mustard Seed

Once Jesus used the example of a mustard seed to teach His disciples about His Kingdom and said, "The grain of mustard seed is one of the smallest grains. But it has the ability to grow quite big. Some varieties of mustard grow into big trees. The branches are strong enough for the birds to nest there. Similarly His kingdom, established by the body of the church, will also grow. By 'church' Lord Jesus meant those who believe in Him will seek the lost, comfort the hurt and point them to Jesus for salvation.

07 The Great Treasure

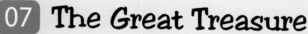

Jesus told a story to his disciples about a man who was working in a field. As he was digging the earth, his spade struck a great treasure. Perhaps it was jewels or coins or precious stones!

The man knew that if he took the treasure it would be like stealing because the field did not belong to him. But if he bought the field, then everything that was in the field would be his, including the treasure. So, he decided to buy the field whatever it cost him. He sold all his belongings and paid for the field. Once, he purchased the field, he happily took out the treasure.

Those who value a relationship with Jesus must be willing to give up their old ways of life. Then, when they believe in Him and follow Him they will find far greater treasure in life than what they had given up.

08 The Pearl of Great Price

Jesus narrated a story about a pearl merchant. He was always looking for the perfect pearl. It is difficult to find pearls as they are formed inside oysters. The merchant travelled places, buying many beautiful pearls. He soon had a wonderful collection.

One day, during one of his business trips, he found a beautiful pearl. It was large and lustrous and absolutely perfect. When he realised how costly it was, he knew he would have to sell his entire collection of pearls to be able to buy just this one pearl! As he knew he would never find another pearl as perfect as this one, he decided to buy it. He sold all his pearls. With the money, he bought the perfect pearl.

By telling this story Jesus wanted to say that people would have to value the Kingdom of Heaven very highly, above and beyond anything they owned or possessed.

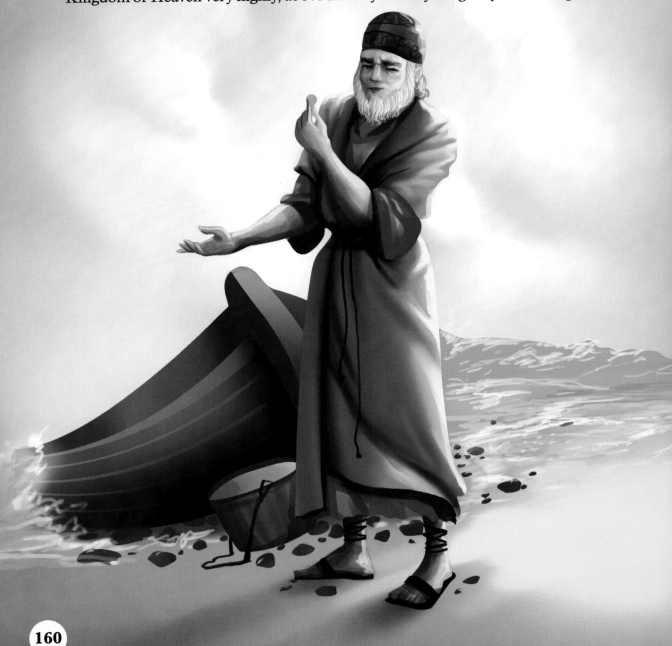

09 The Great Net

Jesus compared the Kingdom of Heaven to a great fishing net once. The net was cast into the sea and when it was full it was dragged to the shore!

There were different types of fish, so, they needed to be sorted out. All the good, edible and worthwhile fish were gathered into vessels. The rest were thrown away.

Jesus explained, "This is exactly how the Kingdom of Heaven would be established. When the time comes for this world to come to an end, the Angels of God will come to separate the good people from the evil ones. All who truly believe in me and follow me would be taken to live in Heaven. But, those who are wicked would be cast into the fires of Hell. In Hell, there will always be great sorrow and separation from God, forever."

10 The Big Feast

Jesus told everyone a story!

There was once a man who invited his friends to a grand feast. After everything was ready, he sent his servants to call his guests. Surprisingly, all his guests gave excuses!

The man who arranged the feast was furious. He told his servants, "Go into the streets and bring the poor and hungry, the blind and lame!"

When the man heard there was still more room at his feast, he sent the servants to bring more people.

None of the first invitees were allowed in. The Jews understood what Jesus was saying. God's Kingdom was not only for Jews but open to anyone who believed in Him.

11 Miracles of Jesus

During Jesus's time on Earth, he travelled to different places and spread the word of God. He also performed miracles when he cured people with severe illness. He made the paralysed walk and the blind see.

On one of these occasions after Jesus had made a paralysed man walk, the priests were shocked and one of them said, "Only God has the right to forgive anyone's sins, how did you do this?"

Jesus smiled and replied, "I am the Son of God who has been sent on this Earth to forgive people's sins."

Turning to the man, he said, "Rise, my son and go home." The paralysed man stood up, to everyone's astonishment and went home praising Jesus and God.

12 Jesus Calls a Tax Collector

The tax collectors were one of the most hated people in any city, as they were known to cheat people and make money out of their taxes. The Jewish priest and the teachers of law considered them as sinners. One day, Jesus approached a tax collector, Matthew, and said "Follow me." Matthew got up and followed Jesus. He invited Jesus to his home and arranged a grand feast. Jesus's disciples and other tax collectors were invited. The teachers of the law complained to the disciples, "Why do you eat and drink with the tax collectors and sinners?"

Jesus answered them, "Those who are healthy do not need to be seen by a doctor; only the sick need a doctor. I have not come for those who are good but for those who are bad, so that they can change from bad and become good."

13 The Centurion's Servant

Once, a Centurion lived in Capernaum. He had a hundred soldiers under his command. One of his servants was very sick. The Centurion wanted him healed. As Jesus entered Capernaum, the Centurion's men pleaded Him to heal the servant.

The Centurion felt he did not deserve to have Jesus enter into his house. Neither did he consider himself worthy to go to Jesus. He sent his friends to tell Jesus not to trouble Himself to come, just speak the word and it would be done as He said. Jesus marvelled at what he heard. He turned to the crowd and said, "I have not found anyone with such great faith, even in Israel." Those who carried this message returned to the Centurion's home and found the servant well.

14 The Daughter of Jairus

A big crowd welcomed Jesus when he returned to Nazareth. A man named Jairus fell at His feet. Jairus was a ruler in the Synagogue. His only daughter was dying. She was about twelve years old. Jairus pleaded with Jesus to come to his house and heal her.

Jesus went. He performed miracles and spoke to the people. Suddenly, someone came from Jairus's house and said, "Don't bother, your daughter is dead."

Jesus said to Jairus, "Don't be afraid; just believe." Jesus went into the house with three disciples. Many people were mourning for her. Jesus told them, "Stop mourning." Then, Jesus took the girl by her hand and said, "Little girl, get up." The girl stood up.

15 A Woman in the Crowd

One day, when Jesus returned to Nazareth, in the crowd was a woman who had a bleeding problem for twelve years. She had spent every penny she had on doctors and no one could heal her. She pressed through the crowd and came up behind Jesus and touched the hem of his robe. Immediately her bleeding stopped.

"Who touched me?" Jesus asked. Peter said, "Master, the people are pressing against you, many would have touched you." But, Jesus said with certainty, "Someone touched me. I felt power going out of Me."

The women who touched Jesus's robe knew she could not remain hidden for long. She came trembling and fell at His feet. In front of everyone in the crowd, she told Jesus why she had touched the edge of his robe and how she was healed, instantly. Then, Jesus told her, "Daughter your faith has healed you. Go in peace."

16 Who is the Most Important?

One day, Jesus heard His disciples argue. Jesus asked them what it was about. They did not reply as they were ashamed of their lack of knowledge. They were arguing about who would be the greatest in the Kingdom of God. Jesus knew that but He wanted to hear them say it.

Jesus said, "If any of you wants the first place in the Kingdom then you should take the last place. You should serve everybody as a servant."

Jesus took a child in His arms and said, "Whosoever receives a child like this, receives me. He who receives me actually receives the one who sent me."

Jesus had come to Earth as a servant to serve the people. Now, He is sitting on the right side of God, the Father in Heaven. He wanted his disciples, too, to have an unselfish attitude.

17 The Miracle of the Loaves and Fish

One day, Jesus and His disciples went to a deserted place in Bethsaida. The crowds followed Him. Jesus spoke to them about the Kingdom of God and healed them. The disciples told Jesus to send the crowd away, so that they could eat and stay in the nearby villages.

Instead, Jesus asked the disciples to give the people something to eat. The disciples replied that a little boy had only five loaves of bread and two fish.

There were about five thousand people. Jesus instructed the disciples to make the people sit in groups of fifty. After they were seated, Jesus took the five loaves of bread and the two fish and prayed over them. He asked the disciples to distribute the food to the people. Amazingly, even after everyone had eaten there were twelve baskets full of leftovers.

18 Jesus Walks on Water

Jesus sent His disciples across the Sea of Galilee and went up the mountain to pray. The winds were strong and the waters were rough. The boat, which carried the disciples, was tossing.

Early in the morning, the people saw someone walking on the water and they got scared.

Jesus said, "It is me, do not be afraid."

Peter replied, "Lord if it is You, call me to join You on the water."

Jesus called Peter, "Come ahead."

Peter started walking on the water towards Jesus. But when he saw the stormy wind, he was scared and started sinking. He cried, "Lord, save me!" Jesus grabbed his hand and said, "Why did you doubt?"

Both of them climbed into the boat and the storm calmed down. The disciples who were in the boat worshipped Jesus, saying, "Truly, You are the Son of God."

19 Madman in the Graveyard

In Gadarenes, a madman lived in the graveyard. He was controlled by unclean spirits. He was very violent. He would shout, day and night, and cut himself with stones. He saw Jesus and asked, "Jesus, what do I do?"

Jesus commanded, "Come out of the man, you unclean spirit." Then Jesus asked him his name.

"Legion, for we are many," he replied.

The spirits asked to be sent into the pigs, grazing on the hillside. Jesus approved. The spirits left the man's body and entered into two thousand pigs, which ran down the hill and drowned in the sea. The man then wore decent clothes and spoke normally. Jesus sent him to his own people to tell them the great things God had done for him.

20 The Widow of Nain's Son

Jesus, His disciples and many other people went to a place called Nain. At the main gate, the dead body of a widow's only son was being carried out. A large crowd led by the sad widow was mourning for the dead boy. Jesus saw the widow and felt very sorry for her. He went up to her and said, "Do not cry."

Jesus touched the coffin and said, "Young man, I say to you, get up."

The boy got up and sat. The mourning stopped. Everybody was talking happily. Jesus gave the young man to his mother. Everyone who saw this miracle was filled with wonder and admiration. They said a great prophet has appeared; God has come to help His people. The news spread all over the country and people started speaking about it.

21 Jesus's Night Visitor

A Pharisee leader named Nicodemus came to meet Jesus at night, so that others would not see him. Jesus told him, "No one can see the Kingdom of God unless he is born again."

Nicodemus could not understand how a grown up could be born again. Jesus explained that everyone should be born of water and spirit; flesh gives birth to flesh and spirit to spirit. Nicodemus said, "How can this be?"

Jesus continued, "If I tell you things that are seen and you do not believe me, how will you believe the unseen things? Everyone who believes in Him will live forever."

God, the Father, loved the whole world so much that He had sent his only Son to set things right.

22 The Woman at the Well

One day, Jesus was passing through Samaria. Tired, He sat beside a well while his disciples went to buy food. A Samaritan woman came to fetch water. Jesus asked her for water. The woman recognised that Jesus was a Jew and was surprised that He spoke to her.

Jesus said, "If only you knew who I was, you would ask me for water. I would give you fresh living water. Those who drink from this well will feel thirty again but those who drink the water I give will never thirst again."

The Samaritan woman asked Jesus for that water. Jesus knew all about her past and present life. Surprised, she thought he was a prophet. The woman said, "I know Christ will come and explain everything."

Jesus said, "I who speak to you am He."

23 The Good Neighbour

One day, a lawyer tested Jesus asking Him what he must do to get eternal life. Jesus said, "Love the Lord, your God, with all your heart and love your neighbour as yourself."

Jesus told him a story explaining who is a neighbour. One day, a man was travelling from Jerusalem to Jericho. Robbers attacked him and took all he had. A priest walked down the road. He saw the traveller lying and went away. Then, a Levite came. He saw the wounded man and walked away. A Samaritan came. He stopped and bandaged the man's wounds. He put him on his donkey and took him to an inn. He paid the innkeeper to take care of him. Jesus asked who the lawyer thought was a neighbour to the wounded one. He replied, "The man who showed kindness!" Jesus instructed that he, too, should do the same.

24 Jesus Heals a Blind Man

One day, Jesus and His disciples saw a blind man. The disciples asked Him whether the man was born blind because of his or his parents' sins. Jesus replied, "It is neither his nor his parents' sins. It had happened so that the work of God might be revealed in his life. As long as it is day, we must do the work for him who sent Me. Night is coming, when no one can work. While I am in the world, I am the light of the world."

Jesus spat on the ground and made clay with the saliva. He applied it to the blind man's eyes and asked him to wash his eyes in the Siloam pool. The man washed his eyes! He could see and joyfully went home. Some people recognised him and he told them that Jesus had healed him. "Where is this man?" they asked. He replied, "I don't know."

25 The Lost Sheep

One day, the tax collectors and sinners had all gathered around Jesus. The Pharisees saw them and murmured, "This man welcomes sinners and eats with them." Then, Jesus told them a story. A man had hundred sheep and one strayed away. Jesus asked them a question. "Would the man leave the ninety-nine on the hills and go looking for the lost sheep?"

He answered his own question, saying, that the man would leave his ninety-nine sheep and go look for the lost sheep. When he finds it, he will joyfully carry it on his shoulders and go home. He would call his friends and celebrate as he has found his poor lost sheep. In the same way, God, our Heavenly Father, is not willing to lose anyone.

26 The Lost Coin

Jesus wanted them to realise that each one was special and God did not want anyone to go the wrong way and perish. Jesus told them another story. A woman had ten silver coins. If she lost even one of the coins, she would light a lamp and sweep the whole house and look for it. She would turn the house upside down. Looking into every nook and cranny, she would not rest till she had found it. Then, when she had found it, she would call all her friends and neighbours, have a feast and celebrate.

She would share her joy with them and say, "Rejoice with me, I have found my lost coin." In the same way, there is great celebration in Heaven among the Angels when even one sinner repents from his bad ways and turns to God.

27 The Lost Son

A rich man had two sons. The younger son demanded his share of property and went to a distant country and spent all his money in careless living. Soon, his money was over and there was famine in the country. He had no food. A man hired him to take care of his pigs. He looked after the pigs and ate the pigs' food. One day, he returned to his father's house to ask for forgiveness. He was willing to work for him as a servant. His father saw him and ran to his son and embraced him.

The son said, "I am not worthy to be called your son." He confessed that he had done wrong. The father arranged for a party to celebrate the return of his son. The best robe, ring and sandals were brought for him. The father said, "My son, who was lost is now found."

28 The Lost Son and His Brother

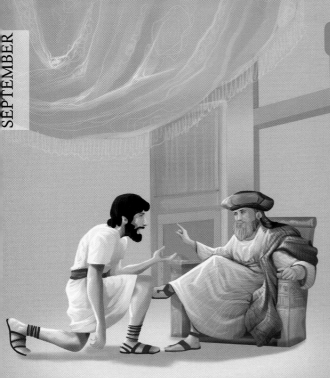

Jesus told the people another story. When the father was celebrating the return of his younger son, the older son came from the fields. A servant told him, "Your brother has returned, and your father has killed the fatted calf because he is back safe and sound."

The angry brother refused to go in. The father went out and pleaded with him. The elder son said to his father, "For many years I have faithfully worked for you! Yet, you never gave me even a young goat to celebrate with my friends. But when this son of yours who finished all your money comes home, you kill the fatted calf for him!" The father replied, "My son, you are always with me, and everything I have is yours. But we have to celebrate because this brother of yours was lost and is found."

29 The Workers and their Pay

Jesus told another parable. One morning, a vineyard owner went to hire labourers. He offered to pay them one dinar for a day's work.

At the end of day, the vineyard owner asked his manager to pay the labourers. He commanded that those hired last would be paid first! All the labourers received exactly the same wage. Those who worked all day were paid the same as those who worked only for a few hours. The workers who started work in the morning were upset.

The vineyard owner asked, "Did you not agree to work for one dinar a day? I have the right to pay everyone what I agreed to pay." Though the Jews were the first people to be chosen of God, those who now believed in Jesus would be first to enter Heaven!

30 The Rich Man

One day, a rich young man fell at Jesus's feet. He said, "Good teacher, what should I do to have eternal life?"

Jesus answered, "Why do you call Me good? No one is good, except God alone. You know the Commandments; do not murder, do not commit adultery, do not steal, do not lie, do not cheat and honour your father and mother!" The man replied, "I have always followed these."

Jesus said, "Go sell everything you have and give it to the poor. You will have treasure in Heaven. Then come and follow me." The man's face fell because he had a lot of wealth. Jesus said, "It is easier for a camel to enter the eye of a needle than for a rich man to enter the kingdom of God."

Jesus explained that man cannot do so alone, but if he accepts Jesus as his saviour then everything is possible.

01 The Largest Gift

Once, Jesus sat down just opposite the money box in the Synagogue. He watched people drop their offerings. Many rich men made a lot of noise dropping the money to get noticed. Then, a poor widow quietly slipped in two small copper coins. Jesus told His disciples, "This poor widow has given a bigger offering than anyone else." All the rest gave out of their abundant wealth but this poor widow gave her everything.

Jesus was teaching His disciples the significance of offerings given for the work of the Lord. Offerings given out of a sacrificial heart have more value than money that is given out of excess. Although the poor widow gave two copper coins, it was of great value because that was all she the money she had. She gave her livelihood. Comparatively, her gift was of greater value than the large amounts the rich dropped in the box.

02 Rich Farmer

Jesus narrated the story of a rich man who had plentiful harvest. This rich man had so much that he did not know where to store it! He thought, I have so many things, I need to break down my old barns and build much larger storehouses! Then I can tell my soul to rest because then I will have enough money to last me for several years! Then, he decided he need not work. Instead, he could simply eat, drink and be merry!

But God said, "Tonight you will die! Now, who will take all the things you so carefully collected and stored?"

Anyone who keeps on thinking of ways and means to hoard more money or things for himself is not rich in the things of God. This man will not enter the Kingdom of God, because money and possessions become his God!

03 Jesus is Transfigured

Once, Jesus, Peter, James and John, climbed up a high mountain. Suddenly, Jesus was transformed from an ordinary man to a God-like being. His face was shining like the sun and His clothes were dazzling white like light. Then Moses and Elijah appeared and the two were speaking with Jesus.

Suddenly a big cloud emerged and they heard a voice, "This is my Son, whom I love. Listen to Him."

The disciples fell to the ground, frightened. They knew that Jesus was the Messiah. Then, Jesus touched them and said, "Get up. Do not be afraid."

When they got up, they saw Jesus alone. Jesus told them not to tell anyone about it until He rose from the dead. They wondered what He meant!

04 The Desperate Father

When Jesus descended the mountain, a crowd saluted him. A worried-looking man said, "Master, I brought my deaf and dumb son to your disciples. He has an evil spirit, which makes him fall, grind his teeth and froth at the mouth. He is very weak. But your disciples could not heal him."

Jesus said, "Oh! faithless ones, how long will I stay with you? Bring the child here!" The boy had another fit. Jesus felt great pity. "Please have mercy and help us!" the father cried. Jesus said, "If you believe, all things are possible!"

Immediately, the father cried, "Lord, I believe! Help me!" Jesus commanded the spirit to come out and never to return again! Again, the boy was thrown and lay like dead. Jesus lifted him up fully healed! When the disciples questioned Jesus why they could not heal him, Jesus replied, "Such healing happens by prayer and fasting."

05 Jesus, the Friend of Children

Once, the disciples asked Jesus, "Who is the greatest in the Kingdom of Heaven?"

Jesus said, "Unless you become like a little child, you cannot enter the Kingdom of Heaven. They have some good qualities unlike adults. They have very strong faith. It is more difficult for adults to have implicit faith."

Jesus added, "Whoever humbles himself like a child will be the greatest in the Kingdom of Heaven. If anyone receives a little child in My name, he receives Me."

Jesus was very fond of children and would often take them in His arms and bless them.

06 The Unforgiving Servant

Once, Peter asked if he should forgive someone, seven times. Jesus replied, "No, seventy times seven." Jesus explained with a parable.

Once, a servant had borrowed ten thousand dinars from his master and was not able to return it. So, the servant begged his master for some time. The master had mercy on him and cancelled the whole debt. Now, that servant met his friend who had borrowed only a hundred dinars from him. The servant angrily demanded his money. The friend begged for time but the servant did not show any pity and threw him into prison.

When the master heard this, he called the wicked servant, saying, "You, wicked servant! I pitied you and cancelled your debt. Should you not have done the same?" The servant was also thrown into prison till he paid back the master. Similarly God will not forgive us if we do not forgive others.

07 Two Blind Men Healed

Wherever Jesus travelled, crowds followed Him. One day, as He walked away from Jericho, a huge crowd followed Him. Two blind men were sitting along the way. They heard the sound of a big crowd following Jesus and knew that Jesus was coming. They did not want to lose the chance to be healed. They started shouting, "Have mercy on us, O Lord, Son of David!" The crowds scolded them. "Be quiet!"

But the two men shouted even louder, to draw Jesus's attention. Jesus heard their cries. He stopped and stood still. Everyone fell silent. Seeing them, Jesus was moved with compassion. Jesus called them, "What would you like me to do for you?" The blind men could not believe it! Jesus was actually speaking to them!

"Lord open our eyes!" they begged. Jesus touched their eyes. They, at once, received their sight. Joyfully they followed Him!

08 Separating Sheep from Goats

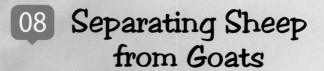

At His second coming, Jesus will return as King. Like a shepherd separating the sheep from goats, He will separate the good and bad people. He will bless the sheep and give them the Kingdom as their inheritance. He will say, "I was hungry and you fed me; thirsty and you gave me a drink; a stranger and you invited me in. You clothed me and looked after me when I was sick. You visited me in prison."

They will respond, "When did we do all this, Lord?" Jesus will answer, "Every time you did these good deeds for someone, you actually did it for me." He will curse the goats and send them to eternal hell fire prepared for the devil. The King will say, "When you refused kindness to someone, you actually were ignoring me." Those who did not follow Jesus will be sent to suffer eternal punishment while His followers will receive eternal life.

09 The Lady's Act of Love

One day, Simon, a Pharisee, invited Jesus home. When Jesus was at the dinner table, a sinful lady quietly stood at His feet, behind Him, and with tears streaming down her cheeks, she washed His feet.

Simon thought if Jesus were a real prophet He would have never let her touch Him. Jesus understood that and said, "Simon, consider two debtors. If one owed five hundred silver pieces and the other fifty and neither could repay, and if the master cancelled their debts who would be more grateful?" Simon answered, "The one who had a larger debt."

"Yes, this lady has been forgiven for many sins. So, she is grateful." Jesus said, "This lady loves Me, she washed, dried and anointed My feet. Woman, I forgive you your sins."

10 Jesus Blesses the Little Ones

The Lord Jesus always spent much time with people, teaching, healing and performing miracles. Crowds of people followed him, everywhere. News about Jesus and His ministry had spread far and wide. Now, mothers in the crowd had brought their little children along. They had hoped that Jesus would touch them and bless them.

The disciples got annoyed and chased them away. Jesus was very angry with His disciples when He saw them and scolded those who brought the children. He told them, "Do not stop the children from coming to Me. The Kingdom of God belongs to those who are like children." The Lord Jesus told all those around Him, "The truth is, unless everyone accepts the Kingdom of God like a child does, they cannot enter it."

11 Jesus Heals the Lepers

On his journey to Jerusalem, Jesus entered a city and ten men, who had leprosy, saw Him.

They called out to Jesus from a distance, "Jesus have pity on us."

Jesus saw them and said, "Go! Show yourselves to the priest."

In those days, the priest had to approve if the lepers could be healed. The lepers listened to Jesus and went to the priest. On the way, they were healed. One of them came back and praised Jesus and thanked Him. He asked Jesus, "How did this miracle happen? How did we get healed so fast?" Jesus touched him and said, "Get up and go, your faith has healed you."

12 Jesus, the Good Shepherd

Jesus told His disciples that He is like the Good Shepherd.

The watchman of Kingdom of Heaven opens the gate only for the Good Shepherd. The sheep hear the Shepherd's voice and listen to Him. He leads them out and they follow Him as they know Him.

A good shepherd will do everything to protect His sheep. Even so much as to lay down his life. A hired man leaves the sheep and runs away when he sees a wolf.

Jesus knows His sheep and they know Him. He will be with them forever, and will not abandon them in the face of adversity. One day, the flock will have only one shepherd.

Jesus, came to the world to lay down His life for everyone else.

13 Jesus, the True Vine

Jesus told his disciples that He is the Real Vine and the Father is the Gardener. The Father cuts off the branches, which do not bear any fruit. The branches which bear fruit He prunes so that they produce more fruit.

The Word of God has already pruned the disciples. They are like the branches. A branch cannot grow on its own without the main plant. Jesus instructs the disciples to remain with the Vine who is Jesus. Then, Jesus will remain with them.

We are the disciples of Jesus. So, we must remain faithful to Jesus and He will live in us. Without the Lord Jesus, we cannot do anything good. But, if we live by the Word of God, we can ask for anything in Jesus's name and it shall be ours. When we bear much fruit, the Father will be glorified and the world will know that we are His disciples.

14 Jesus Prays for the Disciples

Jesus prays to the Father for His disciples. The character of God has been revealed and the message of the Father has been given to them. Jesus specifies that He is praying only for the disciples. He reaffirms that all He has is the Father's and all the Father has is His.

Jesus is not going to be in the world but was going back to Heaven. He asks the Father to protect the disciples so that they may be one as the Father and He are one. Jesus had protected all but one of them with the power of His name. Jesus asked the Father to protect them from evil and sanctify them by His Word. Just like the Father sent Jesus into the world, the disciples have been sent on a mission.

15 The Fig Tree without Figs

Jesus told a parable to explain that unless people turned to God in repentance, they would die. Once, a man planted a fig tree in his vineyard. One day, he told the Gardener, "I have been coming here for three years to see if this fig tree has borne any fruit. But there has not been a single fruit since it has been planted. Cut it down. Do not waste good ground on it any longer." The Gardener replied, "Please let the tree grow for one more year. I will dig around it and manure it. Next year, if the fig tree does not bear any figs, I shall cut it down. But if it does bear fruit I shall not cut it."

The owner represents God who wants people to repent from sin. Jesus is the Gardener who nurtures and cares for it. The fig tree symbolises the people.

183

16 The Wise and the Foolish Virgins

Jesus compared the Kingdom of Heaven to ten virgins, who went to meet the bridegroom carrying lamps. Only five wise virgins carried oil in jars, along with the lamps. The bridegroom arrived at midnight. The virgins woke up and trimmed their lamps. Then, the foolish virgins said to the wise ones, "Please give us some of your oil; our lamps are going out."

The wise virgins replied, "Sorry! We cannot! We do not have enough oil for both us and you. Go and buy oil for yourselves." While the foolish virgins went out to buy oil, the wise virgins went to the wedding banquet. Then, the door was closed. The foolish virgins returned and wanted to be let in. But, they were not allowed in. Jesus warned people to be ready at all times. No one knows when Jesus will return to take His followers with Him to Heaven.

17 The Three Kinds of Servants

The Kingdom of Heaven is also compared to a man who went on a journey. Before his journey, he gave some money to his servants according to their ability. The servant with five talents invested the money and got five more talents in return.

The one with two talents also got two more. But, the servant who got one talent buried it. The master returned and asked for an account. Two servants brought back double. The master was pleased and said, "Well done. You have been faithful with few things." The servant with one talent brought it back. The master was angry and said, "You should have put my money in the bank. I would have earned interest." The useless servant was thrown into outer darkness.

18 Man up a Tree

One day, Jesus was passing through Jericho. A wealthy tax collector called Zacchaeus wanted to see Jesus. He was short and so, climbed up a sycamore-fig tree. When Jesus reached the tree, He stopped. He looked up and called out, "Zacchaeus come down now. I must stay in your house, today." Zacchaeus gladly welcomed Jesus into his home.

No one liked tax collectors because they became rich by cheating people. However, after Jesus spent time with him, Zacchaeus was a changed man. He promised Jesus to give half his wealth to the poor and return four times the amount to anyone whom he had cheated. Jesus said, "Today salvation has come to this house, because this man, too, is a son of Abraham, for the Son of Man came to seek and to save the lost."

185

19 Beggar by the Wayside

Jesus and his disciples, followed by a large crowd, were leaving Jericho. Bartimaeus, a blind man was sitting by the highway and begging. Bartimaeus shouted, "Jesus, Son of David, have mercy on me."

Jesus heard him and stopped. He said, "Call him." The people told blind Bartimaeus, "Cheer up! On your feet now, He is calling you."

Bartimaeus threw off the cloak he was wearing and came to Jesus. Jesus asked him, "What do you want me to do for you?"

"Rabbi, I want to see," replied Bartimaeus. Rabbi means teacher in Hebrew. Jesus said, "Go, your faith has healed you."

Immediately, Bartimaeus was healed and was able to see.

20 The Most Important Things

Jesus was very close to a family in Bethany—two sisters, Mary and Martha, and their brother Lazarus. Jesus and His disciples were passing by Bethany so they visited Martha. Martha welcomed them. Mary, her sister, dropped all her work and sat at the feet of Jesus.

Martha was a good hostess. She was busy getting things ready. She did not sit and even asked her sister to help her. So, Martha asked Jesus, "Lord, do You not care that Mary has left me alone to do the work? Please tell her to help me."

"Martha, you are worried about many things. But there is only one important thing that is needed. Mary has chosen it and that will not be taken away from her," said Jesus. He was making Martha understand that we need to give more importance to our spiritual needs, than our physical bodies needs like food.

21 Illness of a Friend

Lazarus, the brother of Mary and Martha, was very ill. Worried, his sisters sent word to Jesus, "Lord, the one You love is sick."

Jesus said, "This sickness will not end in death. It is for God's glory so that God's Son may be glorified through it."

After two days, Jesus told His disciples, "Lazarus has fallen asleep; but I am going there to wake him up." Jesus meant that Lazarus was dead and He was going to raise him. But His disciples thought Lazarus was sleeping. "Lord, if he is sleeping, he will recover," they said.

Jesus told them, "Lazarus is dead, and for your sake, I am glad I was not there, so that you may believe. But now let us go to him." Thomas doubted Jesus and said to the others, "Let us also go with Jesus."

22 Jesus at Bethany

When Jesus reached Bethany, Lazarus was already in the tomb for four days. Martha went to meet Him, but Mary stayed at home. "Lord, if You had been here, my brother would not have died. But I know that even now God will give You whatever You ask," said Martha. Jesus said, "Your brother will rise again."

Martha thought Jesus meant the resurrection on the last day. Martha returned and told Mary, "The Teacher is here, and is asking for you." Mary went to meet Him. The Jews, comforting Mary, thought she was going to the tomb and followed her. Mary fell at His feet and cried. Jesus was very upset when he saw them crying. Some Jews even saw Jesus crying and said, "See, how he loved him!"

23 Alive Again!

Jesus was terribly sad at the death of Lazarus. He went with His disciples to Lazarus' tomb. The tomb was a cave, closed with a stone. "Take away the stone," said Jesus.

"But, Lord," said Martha, "he has been there for four days and by now there will a bad smell."

Jesus said, "Did I not tell you that if you only believed, you would see the glory of God?" The stone was removed. Jesus looked up and prayed, "Father, I thank You for hearing Me. I say this for the benefit of the people standing here, that they may believe that You sent Me."

Jesus called, loudly, "Lazarus, come out!"

Lazarus came out. Many Jews saw what Jesus did and believed in Him.

24 Jesus Enters Jerusalem

Jesus and His disciples were on their way to Jerusalem. When they were close to Bethany, Jesus sent two of his disciples into the village.

He told them, "Go to the village ahead of me. Just as you enter it, you will find a colt tied there. Untie it and bring it here. If anyone asks you, why are you doing this just tell them, The Lord has need of it, and will send it back soon."

The two disciples found the colt, untied it and spread their cloaks over it for Jesus to sit. Jesus then rode into Jerusalem, triumphantly as a king. The people who stood by the gate of the city to welcome Jesus shouted, "Blessed is He who comes in the name of the Lord! Blessed is the coming kingdom of our father David!"

25 Jesus in the Temple

Jesus entered the temple in Jerusalem and saw everything. Jesus saw animals being sold for sacrifice, people buying and selling things, and money changers doing currency exchange. It was noisy and crowded. Jesus angrily began chasing all of them out!

Jesus overturned the tables of the money changers and the benches of those selling doves. He did not allow anyone to carry goods through the temple courts. He taught the people by saying, "Is it not written: 'My house will be called a house of prayer for all nations?' But you have made it a den of robbers!"

The chief priests and the teachers of the law were angry with Jesus. They wanted to have him killed as they were afraid of him. The whole crowd was amazed at His teaching. In the evening, Jesus and his disciples left the city.

26 Preparing the Passover Meal

It was the first day of the Jewish Feast. The Passover lamb was to be sacrificed on that day. Jesus's disciples asked Him where He wanted to eat the Passover meal. He sent two disciples into the city with instructions to meet a man carrying a jar of water. They were to follow him to a house. The disciples were to meet the owner of the house and tell him, "The Teacher asks: Where is My guest room, where I may eat the Passover with My disciples?"

The disciples did what Jesus had asked them to do and the owner of the house showed them a large room. That was where the disciples were asked to prepare for the Passover feast.

In the evening, Jesus and His twelve disciples arrived for the feast. This was the last meal Jesus had with His disciples before He was betrayed.

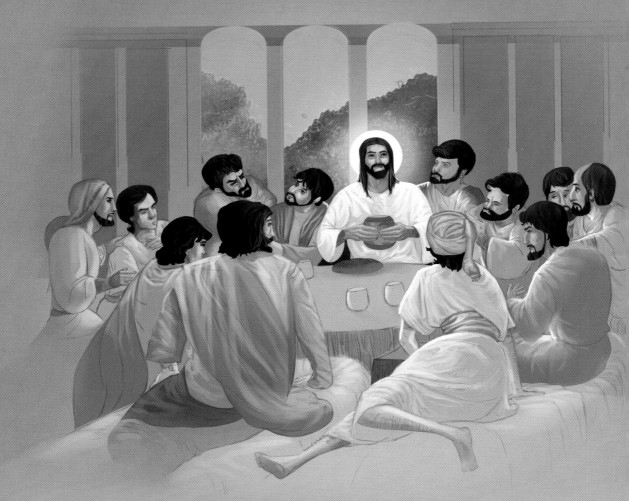

27 The Last Supper

Jesus with His disciples sat down for the Passover meal. The disciples were worried that someone wanted to kill Jesus. Jesus looked around at His disciples and said, "One of you will betray me!" The disciples were shocked! Each one asked Jesus, "Is it I, Lord?"

Jesus said, "The one to whom I offer bread, after dipping it, he will be the one!"

Then, Jesus broke the bread, blessed it and shared it with His disciples, "Take, eat! This is my body, which will be broken for you." He took a cup of wine, thanked God for it and said, "This is my blood. It will be poured out for you, so that your sins will be forgiven."

Then He gave a piece of bread dipped in wine to Judas and said, "Whatever you are going to do, please do it quickly!" No one understood how any disciple could betray Jesus. This meal is referred to as 'The Last Supper' and was Jesus's last meal before His crucifixion.

28 Jesus Washes His Disciples' Feet

After the meal had ended, Jesus got up from the table, filled a basin with water and began to wash the feet of His disciples. Simon Peter asked, "Why are you washing my feet?"

Jesus replied, "If I do not wash you, you have no part with Me. Who has had a bath, only the feet need washing."

Then, He changed His clothes and asked them, "Do you know what I have done for you? If you call me Lord and Master, and have allowed me to wash your feet, then you must wash one another's feet." The servant is not greater than the Lord, nor is the person who is sent greater than the one who sent him.

29 The Garden of Gethsemane

Jesus told Simon Peter that before the sun rises the next day, he would deny Him three times. When Simon Peter protested, Jesus said that all the other disciples would leave Him and run away.

That night, Jesus and His disciples crossed the Kidron brook and entered the Garden of Gethsemane. Jesus told Peter, James and John, "I am sad and my heart is sorrowful. Keep watch and pray." Jesus walked ahead and prayed, "Father, I ask you to help me follow your instructions."

Jesus went back to His disciples and found them sleeping instead of praying. Jesus woke them up, saying, "The time has come for me to be betrayed. Let us go! The one who will betray me is ready."

30 The Arrest and Trial of Jesus

Judas Iscariot brought the soldiers and servants of the high priest with him to the Garden of Gethsemane. They came with torches and weapons.

Jesus asked them, "Who are you looking for?"

They said, "Jesus of Nazareth."

Jesus said, "I am Jesus of Nazareth."

But, they fell on to the ground. Simon Peter pulled out His sword and cut off the servant's ear. Jesus said to Peter, "Put away your sword."

Jesus then healed the servant's ear with His hand. The soldiers bound Jesus and took him away. Peter and another disciple followed. They took Jesus to Annas, the high priest. He questioned Jesus about His disciples and about His teachings. They were worried about his growing band of followers. Jesus told them how He had always preached openly. He had done nothing wrong. A servant struck Him with his palm. Then, Annas had Jesus bound and sent Him to Caiaphas, the governor, for further questioning.

31 Peter Denies Jesus

Simon Peter waited outside in the courtyard where a fire was burning. Simon Peter sat down with the other servants to warm himself.

A servant girl noticed Simon Peter and asked whether he had been with Jesus, but Simon Peter, out of fear of being beaten up or imprisoned, said, "Woman, I do not know Him."

Later that night, a man saw Simon Peter and said, "You are one of them."

Again Simon Peter said, "No, I am not."

Later, another man said, "You are a Galilean. You are with him." Simon Peter, angrily, said, "I do not know whom you are speaking about."

Just as, he was speaking, a rooster crowed. Jesus, who was being escorted by the soldiers, turned and looked straight at Simon Peter. At once, Simon Peter, filled with shame and sorrow, recalled the words of Jesus, "Before the rooster crows, you will disown me three times."

Simon Peter was very sad. He went out and wept bitterly.

01 Jesus Stands Before Pilate

After Jesus's trial was over, He was taken to Pilate, the Roman Governor.
The governor asked Jesus if He was the King of the Jews, to which Jesus replied, "Yes!"

The chief priests accused Him of many things. Jesus remained silent. Pilate said that he could not find anything wrong with Jesus, but the priests said that He was trying to change the people of Judea with His teachings and that He had started in Galilee.

When Pilate discovered that Jesus was a Galilean, he sent Jesus to Herod who governed Galilee. Herod was delighted. He had heard of Jesus's miracles. He asked Jesus many questions, but Jesus remained silent. They sent Jesus back to Pilate. Pilate wanted Jesus to be beaten and then set free. But, the priests wanted Him to be crucified. Pilate tried to free Jesus but the priests disagreed.

Pilate handed Jesus to them to do whatever they wanted.

02 Carrying the Cross

The Roman soldiers whipped Jesus and led Him into the Praetorium, a hall. They made a crown of thorns and pressed it on to His head, mocking Him, "Hail! The King of the Jews!"

They hit Him on the head and spat on Him.

They brought forth a huge wooden cross and gave it to Jesus. He carried it to Golgotha, which meant 'place of a skull'. His loyal disciples followed Him.

They gave Jesus some wine mixed with myrrh to drink, to deaden His pain, but He refused. Jesus got weakened from the walk and the constant whipping. He could not carry the heavy wooden cross anymore.

The Centurion, a Roman commander, called to a man, Simon of Cyrene, who lifted the cross from Jesus's shoulders onto his own, walking with Jesus the rest of the way to Golgotha.

03 The Death of Jesus

At Calvary, they nailed Jesus to the cross between two criminals. Pilate wrote the title, "Jesus of Nazareth, the King of the Jews," in three languages, Hebrew, Greek and Latin, and placed it on top of the cross.

Jesus gave His mother to one of His disciples, John's care. Then Jesus bowed his head and called out, "Father, I place my spirit in your hands." Saying so, Jesus breathed his last breath.

The skies darkened and the Earth shook. A soldier pierced Jesus's side. Blood and water flowed out. Joseph of Arimithaea and Nicodemus took Jesus's body down and embalmed it, wrapping it in white linen with spices. They laid Him in a tomb in a garden.

04 Mary in the Garden

The next morning, on the first day of the week, Mary Magdalene, a follower, visited Jesus's tomb. The stone at the mouth of the tomb had been rolled away! His body was missing! Frightened, she ran to tell His disciples. Peter and another disciple came running and went inside the cave to check. Mary remained outside, tears running down her cheeks. Suddenly, she heard a voice, "Why are you crying?" She turned to see an angel.

Mary replied, "Someone took away Jesus's body." The angel replied, "That's because He has risen." Mary felt as if someone was standing behind her and turned to see a man, he asked her, "Who are you looking for?" Mary told him everything and said, "I need to find Him."

The man said "Mary!" and she realised who He was. She joyfully exclaimed, "Rabboni!"

Mary ran to tell the disciples that Jesus had truly risen!

05 Jesus is Sighted Again

On the same day, two believers of Jesus were travelling to the village of Emmaus. They were in deep conversation. A stranger walked up to them and asked the two disciples, "What are you talking about?" One of the believers, Cleopas, answered, "Do you not know about Jesus of Nazareth?"

Assuming the stranger had not heard about Jesus, he spoke about Jesus, his miracles and teachings, his trial and death. He also told the stranger about Jesus's resurrection. The stranger asked them, "Did the prophets not tell you that Christ will suffer before entering His glory?"

When they reached the village, the believers invited the stranger for supper. The stranger accepted the invitation and when sat down with them and broke the bread, he thanked God and shared the bread with the disciples. That very moment, the believers realised that the stranger was no other than Jesus himself. But when they blinked and looked again, He had vanished. Excitedly, they returned to Jerusalem and informed the other eleven disciples about Jesus.

06 Thomas Doubts

Ten disciples locked themselves in the room. Suddenly, Jesus appeared before them. The disciples were frightened to see Jesus and thought that He is a ghost. Jesus reassured them, "Look at my wounds. I am no ghost."

He explained that He had to fulfil the prophecy about him. He had to suffer and die before he could rise after three days. "Just like My Father sent me, I am sending You. Receive the Holy Spirit!" Saying so, He breathed on them and left suddenly.

A disciple, Thomas, was not present in that room when Jesus had appeared and refused to believe what others told him. After a week, when the twelve disciples were in a locked room, Jesus appeared again. He showed his wounds to Thomas and said, "Stop doubting and believe." Thomas bowed down to Him and cried, "My Lord and My God!"

07 Jesus Restores Peter

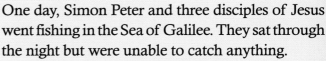

One day, Simon Peter and three disciples of Jesus went fishing in the Sea of Galilee. They sat through the night but were unable to catch anything.

On reaching the shore, they saw a stranger who asked, "Did you catch any fish?" The disciples shook their heads. The stranger said, "Throw the net on the right side of the boat." The disciples went back to the sea and did just that. The net was full of fish. The disciples realised that the stranger was Jesus. Simon swam to the shore and fell down at Jesus's feet. Jesus asked him thrice, "Do you love me?" Simon replied, "Yes, I do, my Lord!" (As Simon Peter had denied Jesus three times.) Jesus told Simon Peter, "Take care my sheep, my people, when I am gone."

After Jesus had ascended to Heaven, Simon Peter, preaching the gospel to every place God sent him.

08 The Ascension

Jesus appeared to His disciples for forty days after He had risen from the dead! He explained many things to them about the Kingdom of God and told them to stay in Jerusalem and wait for a special gift—the gift of the Holy Spirit who would live within them and give them power to be His witnesses. He wanted them to tell everyone how He had died for them and that they were to baptise all those who believed in Him.

He was taken up to Heaven right in front of them. A huge cloud hid Him from their sight and they could not see Him anymore!

Suddenly, two Angels appeared and assured them that Jesus would come back again, someday, in exactly the same way that they had seen Him go up to Heaven.

09 Peter, the Leader

Jesus told Simon Peter that He wanted him to preach His word. Although Peter had denied Him, Jesus still wanted him to do His work.

The word Gospel means 'good news'. The good news was that Jesus, God's Son, had come to Earth, did miracles, and finally died on the cross as a sacrifice for the sins of the whole world. Anyone who believed in Jesus would never perish, but would live forever with Him in Heaven. Jesus also told Peter that when his preaching work was done, he would be killed. Jesus ended His talk with Peter by using the same words with which He had first called Peter. "Follow Me!"

Peter faithfully followed Jesus all his life, preaching the gospel.

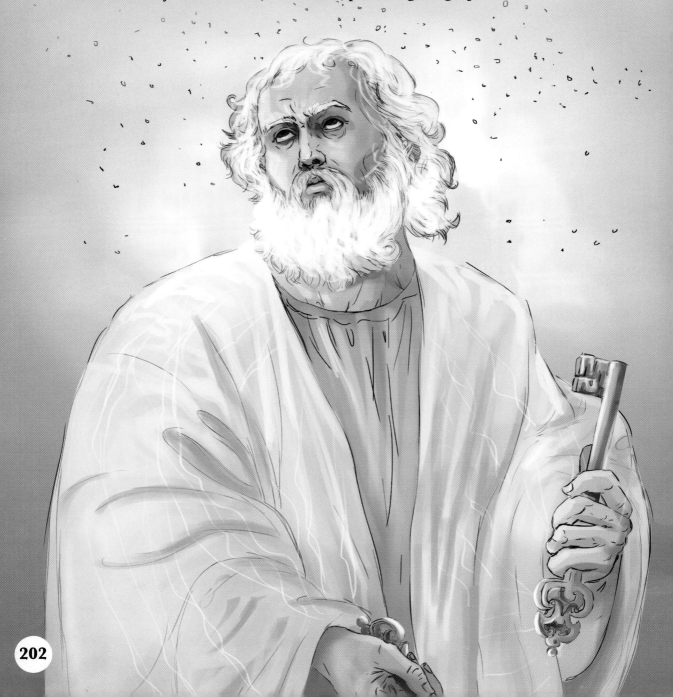

10 Pentecost

After Jesus ascended to Heaven, the eleven disciples gathered in a house and decided that they will welcome one more disciple from the believers. (Jesus had originally chosen twelve disciples; Judas Iscariot betrayed Jesus and the disciples were eleven in number). Matthias was chosen to become one of His disciples (also known as 'Apostles').

On the day of Pentecost, fifty days after Jesus's resurrection, a great gust of wind blew in the house from Heaven and tongues of fire flickered over the heads of the disciples, and they were filled with the Holy Spirit. They realised that they could communicate in different languages from other lands. The news spread like wildfire to many countries and people came to listen to the Apostles speak about God in their own language. This event marks the beginning of the Christian church.

11 Peter Proclaims the Good News

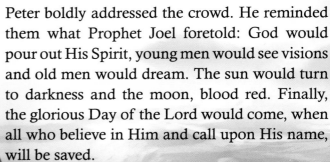

Peter boldly addressed the crowd. He reminded them what Prophet Joel foretold: God would pour out His Spirit, young men would see visions and old men would dream. The sun would turn to darkness and the moon, blood red. Finally, the glorious Day of the Lord would come, when all who believe in Him and call upon His name, will be saved.

Peter preached his first sermon, telling them how God had sent His Son, Jesus, to save mankind from sin. Jesus performed miracles wherever He went. But the Jews crucified Him. God raised Him from the dead! Jesus returned to Heaven. But, Jesus will come one day to take all His followers to Heaven, to live with Him, eternally.

That day three thousand people believed in Jesus and were baptised.

12 The Lame Man Walks

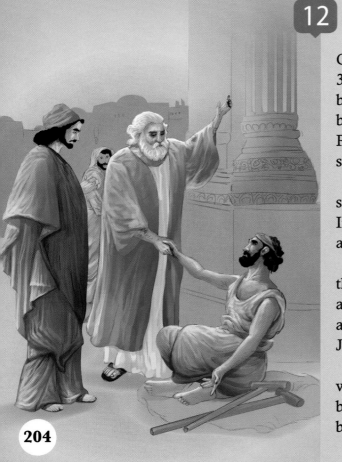

One day, Peter and John went to the temple at 3 o'clock, the prayer time. A man crippled from birth was carried to the temple gate and left to beg there. He asked Peter and John for money. Peter and John looked straight at him. Peter said, "Look at us!"

The man looked. Peter said, "I do not have silver and gold, but I will give you what I have. In the name of Jesus Christ of Nazareth, get up and walk!"

Taking him by the right hand, Peter helped the lame man to his feet. The crippled man's feet and ankles grew strong. He jumped to his feet and began to walk. He accompanied Peter and John into the Temple, praising God.

When the people recognised him, they were amazed to see him walking! "Repent and believe in Jesus," Peter said, "and your sins will be forgiven!"

13 Peter and John are Arrested

People were astonished to see the beggar and went to Peter and John in Solomon's Colonnade. Peter said to them, "Men of Israel, why does this surprise you? Why do you stare at us as if by our own power we have made this man walk? You disregarded Jesus, the Holy and Righteous One. You crucified the Author of Life, but God raised him from the dead! By faith in the name of Jesus, this man whom you see was healed. It is the power of Jesus's name."

Peter and John proclaimed that Jesus had risen from the dead. The priests, the captain of the temple guard and the Sadducees seized them, and put them in jail. They would be taken before the Sanhedrin or Council, the next day.

But, that day the number of believers increased to about five thousand.

14 The Trial of the Disciples

The next day, the rulers, elders and teachers of law met in Jerusalem. Annas, the high priest, Caiaphas and other members of his family were also present. Peter and John were brought before them. The Council asked them, "By what power or what name did you do this?"

Peter was filled with the Holy Spirit and replied, "Rulers and elders of the people, if we are being called to account for the kindness shown to a cripple and how he was healed, then know this, you and all the people of Israel: It is by the name of Jesus Christ of Nazareth that this man stands before you healed."

They commanded Peter and John never again to preach in the name of Jesus. Peter and John replied, "You must judge for yourselves whether it is right for us to obey you rather than God."

The elders could not decide on their punishment. They were released.

15 The Couple who Lied

The early Christians sold their property and the money went into a common fund. They lived together. Ananias and his wife, Sapphira, sold some property. But they kept some money for themselves. The Holy Spirit revealed this to Peter. Peter asked, "Ananias, how did Satan fill your heart so that you could lie to the Holy Spirit and keep back some money for yourself? Why did you do this? You have not lied to men, but to God!" Ananias dropped dead. Three hours later, Sapphira, unaware, came in. Peter asked her, "Tell me, is this the price you and Ananias got for your land?"

She said, "Yes!" Peter asked, "How could you both try to test the Spirit of the Lord? Look! The men who buried your husband are coming to carry you out."

She, too, fell dead. Fear seized the whole church and all who heard about this.

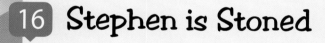

16 Stephen is Stoned

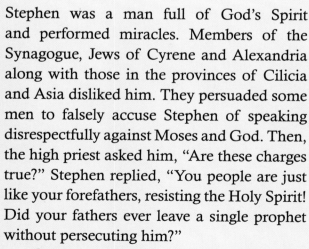

Stephen was a man full of God's Spirit and performed miracles. Members of the Synagogue, Jews of Cyrene and Alexandria along with those in the provinces of Cilicia and Asia disliked him. They persuaded some men to falsely accuse Stephen of speaking disrespectfully against Moses and God. Then, the high priest asked him, "Are these charges true?" Stephen replied, "You people are just like your forefathers, resisting the Holy Spirit! Did your fathers ever leave a single prophet without persecuting him?"

Stephen looked up to Heaven and said, "Look, I see Heaven open! Jesus is standing at God's right hand." They covered their ears, dragged him out of the city and stoned him. Stephen prayed, "Lord Jesus, receive my Spirit. Please do not hold this sin against them." And he died.

17 Simon, the Sorcerer

Simon was a clever man and he lived in Samaria. He practiced sorcery and held the people of Samaria in his power! When Philip arrived in Samaria to preach about the Kingdom of God many believed him and were baptised. Surprisingly, even Simon believed in the Lord Jesus! He was baptised and followed Philip, everywhere.

When the Apostles in Jerusalem heard the good news that Samaria had received the Word of God, they sent Peter and John to Samaria to pray for the people. When Peter and John placed their hands on them, they received the Holy Spirit. When Simon saw that, he wanted to do the same. He offered money to receive that same power!

Peter said, "Your money perishes with you! You cannot buy God's gift with money! Pray that God will forgive your wickedness."

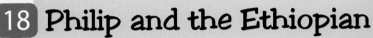

18 Philip and the Ethiopian

One day, an Angel of the Lord told Philip, "Go south to the desert road that connects Jerusalem to Gaza."

On his way, he saw an Ethiopian eunuch, an important official in charge of Queen Candace's treasury. He had worshipped in Jerusalem and was returning to Ethiopia. The Holy Spirit prompted Philip to go to him.

The Ethiopian was reading the prophecy of Isaiah, about someone being led like a sheep to the slaughter, and 'as a lamb before the shearer is silent, He did not open his mouth'.

Philip explained that Isaiah was talking about Jesus who would be crucified. Philip told him to believe in the Lord Jesus to be forgiven of his sins. The Ethiopian asked Philip to baptise him, because he truly believed that Jesus was the Son of God. Immediately, the Holy Spirit took Philip away. The Ethiopian never saw Philip again!

19 Saul Hears a Voice

Saul was a Pharisee who threatened the Apostles. He got letters from the high priest to the Synagogues in Damascus, for permission to arrest people belonging to 'The Way' as Christians were then called!

As Saul neared Damascus, suddenly a light flashed from Heaven and a voice said, "Saul, why are you persecuting Me?"

"Who are you?" asked Saul.

"I am Jesus, whom you are persecuting! Now go into the city. I will tell you what to do." Saul was now blind.

Ananias, a disciple, lived in Damascus. The Lord sent Ananias to Saul of Tarsus, who was chosen to preach to the Gentiles. Placing his hands on Saul, Ananias said, "Brother Saul, the Lord Jesus, who you heard, sent me, so that you may see again and be filled with the Holy Spirit."

Suddenly Saul could see again, he got up and was baptised.

20 Saul Becomes a Christian

Saul began preaching in the Synagogues that Jesus is the Son of God. Astonished, people asked, "Isn't this the same man who destroyed those who taught in Jesus's name in Jerusalem? Did he not come here to take us prisoners to the chief priests?"

Saul preached powerfully. Furious, the Jews conspired to kill him, but Saul discovered their plans. One night, the disciples helped Saul escape, by lowering him in a basket through an opening in the city wall. Saul arrived in Jerusalem and tried to join the disciples, but they did not believe that he had changed.

Barnabas convinced them recounting how the Lord Jesus had spoken to Saul on his journey to Damascus, and how Saul had stayed in Damascus preaching fearlessly in Jesus's name. Later, he boldly debated with the Grecian Jews, who also wanted to kill him.

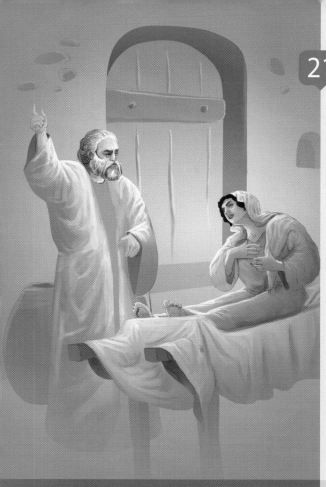

21 Peter Heals Tabitha

In Joppa, a Christian lady called Tabitha was very kind and helped many people. She had a great talent for sewing clothes and she used to sew many coats and garments for those in need.

One day, she died. Her body was washed according to the custom and laid in the upper room. Everybody was mourning around her. When the believers heard Peter was nearby they sent two men to bring him to see Tabitha.

After Peter heard of her kindness and saw the clothes she had made for the poor, he went into the room. Peter told everyone to leave the room. Kneeling down, he prayed and turned to the dead woman and said "Tabitha, get up!" She opened her eyes, looked at Peter. He helped her stand and showed others that she was alive. After that many more people started to believe in Jesus.

22 Peter's Vision

Once, Peter went onto the roof to pray. He felt hungry. Suddenly, Peter saw a vision—Heaven opened and a great sheet tied at four corners, come down to Earth. It was full of four-footed animals, wild beasts, birds and reptiles. A voice said, "Get up, Peter, kill and eat!" Peter replied, "Lord, I have never eaten anything unclean!" The voice said, "What God has cleansed for you, do not call unclean!"

This happened thrice. After a while three men from the centurion arrived. The Holy Spirit said, "Peter, three men are looking for you. Go down with them, for I have sent them." Peter said, "I am the one you are looking for. What do you want?"

They replied, "An Angel told our master, Cornelius, a man respected by Jews, to invite you to his house."

23 Cornelius

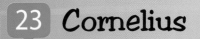

Cornelius was a centurion of the Italian band of soldiers in Caesarea. Once, he saw an Angel in a vision, "Send some men to Jaffa and invite Simon Peter to your home." When Peter came, Cornelius worshipped Peter! Cornelius told Peter about his vision.

Peter told him that it was unlawful for a Jew like him to keep company with a gentile like Cornelius. But God had just showed Peter in his vision of the sheet of animals that God accepts everyone who fears him. Peter told Cornelius how God had sent Jesus, His Son. Jesus did miracles, and healed many. He was crucified but God raised Him on the third day. Peter had witnessed all this. Now Jesus was in Heaven. The Holy Spirit was given to His followers. Cornelius and his family believed. Peter baptised them. They were filled with the Holy Spirit.

24 Saul Begins his Ministry

With the preaching of Peter and other disciples, the church began to grow. Many people turned from their sins and believed in Jesus.

Barnabas was a godly man, full of the Holy Spirit and faith in Lord Jesus. Barnabas went on to Tarsus and brought Saul back with him to Antioch. They joined the local church and preached about Jesus.

For the first time, the believers in Antioch were called Christians, the name by which believers in Christ are called even today.

During the reign of Claudius Caesar Agabus, a prophet, foretold that there would be a world-wide famine. All the disciples decided to send whatever relief they could to those suffering in Judaea. So, they collected money and gave it to Barnabas and Saul. They took it to the elders to distribute it to the needy.

25 Prison Doors Open for Peter

King Herod was arresting the Christians and even killed an Apostle, James. He arrested Peter and imprisoned him. During the feast of the unleavened bread, execution was not permitted. Herod wanted to present Peter to the Jews after Easter.

The night before Peter's trial, he was asleep with two soldiers on either side of him. Peter was tied with two chains, and soldiers guarded the prison door.

Suddenly, the room lit up. An Angel tapped Peter awake, telling him to hurry. Peter's chains simply fell off! The Angel told Peter to put on his clothes and shoes, wrap his cloak around him and follow him. Peter thought that it was a vision. They passed through the guard without being seen. The iron-gate leading into the city swung open on its own! Then the Angel left.

Peter realised that God had sent an Angel to release him.

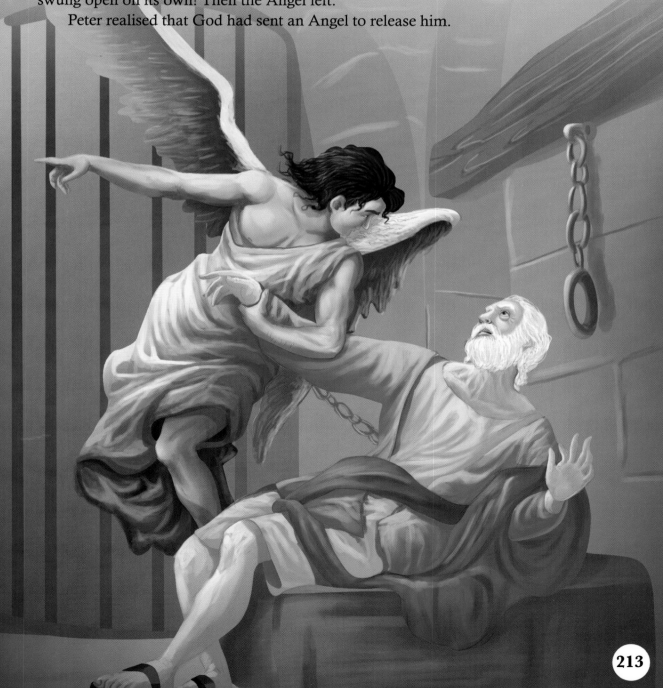

26 Peter's Great Escape

When Peter realised he was free, he went to the house of Mary, John Mark's mother. Many people had gathered there to pray for Peter.

When Peter knocked at their door, a girl named Rhoda came to answer. But, when she recognised Peter's voice, she was so excited she did not open the door. She ran in to tell the others. But they did not believe her. Peter kept on knocking. When they opened the door and saw him, they were astonished. But Peter told them how wonderfully the Lord had sent His Angel to rescue him. He encouraged them to tell James and the other believers what happened.

The next day, there was a great commotion in the prison. The soldiers simply could not understand how Peter had disappeared.

When Herod could not find Peter, he angrily commanded that the guards be put to death.

27 Paul, the Preacher

The church at Antioch was actively working. They had changed Saul's name to it's Roman form, Paul. The Holy Spirit commanded that Barnabas and Paul were chosen for special preaching work. They went preaching through many cities. John Mark too joined them. In Paphos, they met Sergius Paulus, a learned man, who invited them to his home to hear the word of God.

There lived a Jew magician named Elymas.

Paul, filled with the Holy Spirit, said to Elymas, "You son of the devil, Why don't you give up your wicked ways? The hand of the Lord will strike you blind if you don't."

Darkness fell upon Elymas and he became blind. When Sergius Paulus saw this, he believed in the Lord Jesus. Paul and his group went on to Perga. John Mark returned to Jerusalem.

28 The Gods Have Come!

Paul and Barnabas entered the Jewish Synagogue in Iconium and boldly preached. Many Jews and Greeks believed them. But the unbelieving Jews turned the Gentiles against the Apostles. When they all tried to stone them, the Apostles fled to Lystra and Derbe.

At Lystra, Paul saw that a man crippled from birth had faith and commanded, "Stand upright on your feet!" Instantly, he walked. Amazed, everyone began to exclaim in the Lycaonian language, "The Gods have come down to us in the form of men!"

They called Paul, Mercury, the chief speaker and Barnabas, Jupiter!

They brought the priest of the temple of Jupiter with garlands and oxen, ready to offer sacrifices to them. Paul and Barnabas had to stop the people from worshipping them. The Jews who came from Antioch and Iconium persuaded the crowds to stone Paul. They dragged Paul out of the city, thinking he was dead.

29 Judas and Silas are Chosen

The church leaders in Jerusalem sent Judas and Silas along with Paul and Barnabas to Antioch, with this letter:

"Brothers, we send you greetings. We have heard that some people who came from among us have troubled you with words. We have sent Judas and Silas with our beloved Barnabas and Paul. These men have risked their lives for Jesus's sake.

Judas and Silas will teach you the same things, but by word of mouth. The Holy Spirit has led us to instruct you to follow these simple rules. Avoid eating food sacrificed to idols. Do not eat the meat with the blood in it or from strangled animals. Restrain yourself from doing evil deeds. If you avoid doing these, you will fare well. Goodbye."

The believers rejoiced. Judas and Silas taught the believers many things.

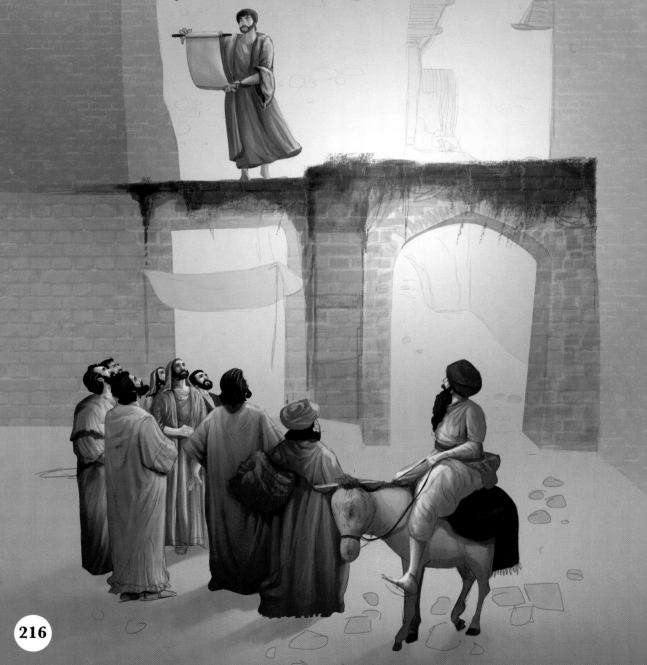

30 Paul and Barnabas Separate

Silas stayed on in Antioch preaching while Judas returned. Paul and Barnabas, too, preached in Antioch. One day, Paul suggested to Barnabas that they travel again to every city they had preached in and check how the new believers were progressing in their faith. Barnabas agreed.

But he wanted to take John Mark along with them. This was the same John who had left them half-way through their preaching ministry earlier, when Paul and Barnabas had visited Paphos. Paul had been upset when John had done that. So, Paul did not want to take John Mark. But Barnabas wanted to give John Mark another chance.

Sadly, both Paul and Barnabas could not come to an agreement. So, they decided to travel in different directions with different companions. Barnabas took John Mark and sailed on to Cyprus. Paul took Silas and travelled through Syria and Cilicia, encouraging and teaching the new believers wherever they visited.

01 Paul Meets Timothy

When Paul arrived at Derbe and Lystra, he met Timothy, a young follower of Jesus. Timothy's mother and grandmother believed in Jesus, but Timothy's father was Greek. These Godly women positively influenced his life.

Paul was very pleased with young Timothy and so, Timothy accompanied Paul and Silas. He proved to be an excellent and useful helper. Paul circumcised him according to the Old Testament Jewish laws because certain believers would not accept him, as his father was Greek. Timothy started preaching God's word. They went through various cities and taught all that Jesus had taught them. The believers were strengthened in the faith, and the church grew.

Paul grew to love Timothy as his own son. When Timothy was ill, Paul cared for him. Later, Timothy stayed with Paul when he was in prison. Truly, Timothy was Paul's great comfort and support.

02 Lydia of Philippi

Paul and his companions reached Philippi, a Roman colony.

On the Sabbath day, they went to the riverside. They saw some women who met there for a prayer meeting. Paul and his friends joined them. Paul explained to them that if they believed in Jesus they could be saved from their sins.

Lydia, a woman who knew about Paul, came to hear him. She was a seller of purple-dyed material from the city of Thyatira. This expensive material was usually worn by high people in society. She worshipped God, but she did not understand Him. As Paul preached, the Lord opened her heart to believe what he said. She accepted Jesus as Lord and was baptised. So, Lydia was the first person to believe in Jesus in Philippi!

03 The Fortune-teller Freed

One day, a slave girl possessed by a demon met Paul and his group. The girl foretold things of the future, so her masters earned money through her fortune-telling. This girl followed Paul and the others and kept repeating, "These men are the servants of the Most High God!" Paul felt sorry for her.

One day, Paul angrily commanded the demon to come out of her. The demon left her body, at once. She could no longer tell the future. Her masters were furious when they understood that they could not earn any more money.

They complained that Paul and his fellow Jews were causing trouble in the city. They were teaching the Roman people, customs that were against their law to practice! The magistrates ordered the crowd to beat up Paul and his companions.

04 Songs and Earthquakes

Paul and Silas were jailed. The jailer thrust them into the inner prison and put their feet in stocks. However, Paul and Silas were not discouraged. At midnight, they were singing praises to God and praying. Suddenly, a great earthquake struck, shaking the prison! All the prisoners' bonds fell off! The horrified jailer woke up and saw the prison doors wide open! Thinking that the prisoners had escaped, he drew his sword to kill himself.

Paul stopped him, "Do not harm yourself, we are all here!" The jailer fell down before Paul and Silas. Bringing them out, he asked, "What must I do to be saved?"

They said, "Believe the Lord Jesus Christ, and you and your household will be saved." The jailer's household believed and were baptised. The jailer washed their wounds, took them home and fed them, rejoicing in his new faith in Jesus!

05 Paul in Athens

When Paul visited Athens, he was moved because of the great idolatry he saw. Paul preached about Jesus, His death and resurrection! But the Athenians did not understand.

Paul went to Mars Hill and saw an altar built to 'the Unknown God!' Paul said that though the Athenians were god-conscious, they were ignorant about the true God!

It was God who ensured that if man should seek Him, man can find Him! God had been patient when people had not sought Him, but now He commands all people everywhere to repent, because He has fixed a day when He will judge the world in righteousness. Everyone will be raised after death because God raised Jesus from the dead.

Some mocked. But others said, "We will hear you again." But unable to bear the ignorance Paul went his way.

06 Paul in Corinth

In Corinth, Paul met a Jew named Aquila, a native of Pontus. Paul preached in the Synagogue every Sabbath, trying to persuade the Jews and Greeks that belief in Jesus was the only way to salvation.

When Silas and Timothy arrived from Msacedonia, Paul was more encouraged to preach, boldly. But his listeners mocked him. Paul angrily said, "You must bear the blame for rejecting Jesus!"

Crispus, the chief ruler of the Synagogue, believed and was baptised with many believers.

One day, the Lord encouraged Paul in a vision, "Do not be afraid, go on speaking and do not be silent, for I am with you. I have many in this city who are My people."

Paul obediently stayed for a year and half, teaching the word of God.

07 Paul and the Tent-makers

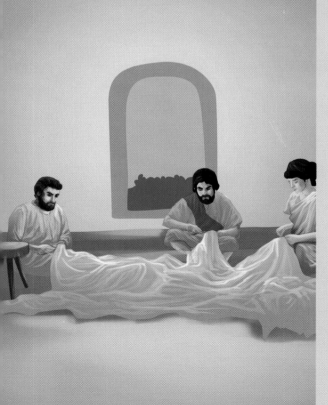

Aquila and his wife Priscilla were tent-makers. Though he was highly learned, Paul too made tents to earn a living. Paul always believed in supporting himself. So, Paul worked along with them.

Paul had always believed and encouraged his fellowmen to labour and toil, when they preached to the people about the word of God. That way neither Paul nor his disciples could be accused of laziness or dependence on others.

Aquila and Priscilla learnt much from Paul. They grew so close to him that they followed him on some missionary journeys. They supported Paul in his preaching work by teaching the young believers who visited their house.

08 Aquila, Priscilla and Apollos

Paul travelled to Ephesus with Priscilla and Aquila. He went on to Galatia to strengthen the believers. Priscilla and Aquila stayed back in Ephesus.

A Jew, Apollos, visited Ephesus. He had studied the scriptures very well and spoke eloquently. But he knew only about the baptism that John, the Baptist had preached. He had not learnt that Jesus was the Saviour.

One day, he preached very passionately in the Synagogue. Priscilla and Aquila were listening. They invited young Apollos home and taught him the way of God more accurately. Apollos quickly learnt all about Jesus. He was now able to persuade the Jews more convincingly by using the scriptures that Jesus was indeed the Messiah.

When Apollos decided to travel further and preach the Gospel, the believers wrote letters, encouraging the disciples there to receive him. Apollos greatly helped in building up the new believers in the faith.

09 Sons of Sceva

God was working extraordinary miracles through Paul. He cured diseases and evil spirits came out of possessed men.

Then, some travelling Jews began to cast out evil spirits, using Paul's name! They drove out devils, saying, "We command you to come out in the name of Jesus, whom Paul preaches."

One day, all the seven sons of Sceva, a Jewish high priest tried the same thing! But the evil spirit jumped on them, screaming, "Jesus I know, and Paul I recognise, but who are you?" The man with the evil spirit overpowered them. They were so terrified that they ran out of the house. Frightened, those who practiced magic arts brought their books together and burnt them. The value of these books was fifty thousand pieces of silver! The Lord Jesus was greatly glorified and the word of God triumphed!

10 The Riot of the Silversmiths

One day, Demetrius, a silversmith, who made shrines and idols of Goddess Diana, gathered the other craftsmen, said, "Men, you know we earn our money from this craft. Paul has persuaded and turned the hearts of many by preaching that gods made with our hands are not gods. Soon both our trade and the temple of our great Goddess Diana may be abandoned and nobody will worship her."

The enraged people shouted, "Great is Diana of the Ephesians!"

They rushed to the public meeting place, dragging Paul's travel companions. Paul wanted to stop them, but he was restrained. Finally, the town clerk calmed the crowd, "These men have neither robbed our churches nor said anything bad about our Goddess. If Demetrius and the craftsmen have any complaints, let them bring the charges to court."

11 Boy Saved in Troas

On the first day of the week, that is the Lord's Day, the disciples gathered together in an upper room to break bread, obeying Jesus's instructions. Paul had to leave the next morning.

So, Paul reminded them how to live their lives, pleasing God. Paul talked till midnight. Among them was a young man named Eutychus. He was sitting at a window and fell asleep. Suddenly, he fell from the window from the third story to the ground below. They thought that Eutychus had died. Paul quickly went down and took him in his arms. Paul said, "Do not be alarmed, for he is not dead. He is alive."

They all came up again. They ate bread together and Paul continued talking with them for a little longer, until daybreak, and then he left. They took young Eutychus away, alive, and happy.

12 Paul Says Goodbye

Paul decided to be in Jerusalem on the Day of Pentecost. He sent for the elders of the church of Ephesus to tell them, the words of God and to wish them goodbye. He said that the Holy Spirit had told him of the suffering he still had to face, but he was not afraid. He wanted to finish his life on Earth with joy.

Paul commanded them to look after the young churches, feeding the 'sheep' whom Jesus had saved by His own death. Paul told them to beware of 'wolves' that would harm the 'flock' as Paul himself had done with prayers and tears, for the past three years.

Paul advised them that it was more blessed to give than to receive and prayed with them. They all wept and kissed Paul, knowing they would never see him again. They escorted him to the ship and said goodbye to him.

13 Paul in Jerusalem

In Caesarea, Paul stayed with Philip, the Evangelist. Agabus, a prophet, told Paul that he would be imprisoned. The believers wept, advising Paul not to go to Jerusalem. As Paul wasn't afraid, he went saying, "The Lord's will be done."

One day, when he was in the temple in Jerusalem, the Jews stirred up the people by saying, "This man has spread wrong teachings everywhere and has even brought the Greeks into the Temple to pollute it!" Angrily, they dragged Paul out of the temple and beat him. The chief captain brought centurions to control the mob, and took Paul into the castle.

From the castle steps, Paul spoke in Hebrew to the Jews about how Jesus had encountered him on the Damascus road. The captain ordered Paul to be scourged. Paul asked, "Can you lawfully scourge me, a free-born Roman citizen, without a trial?" The captain ordered Paul to face the Council.

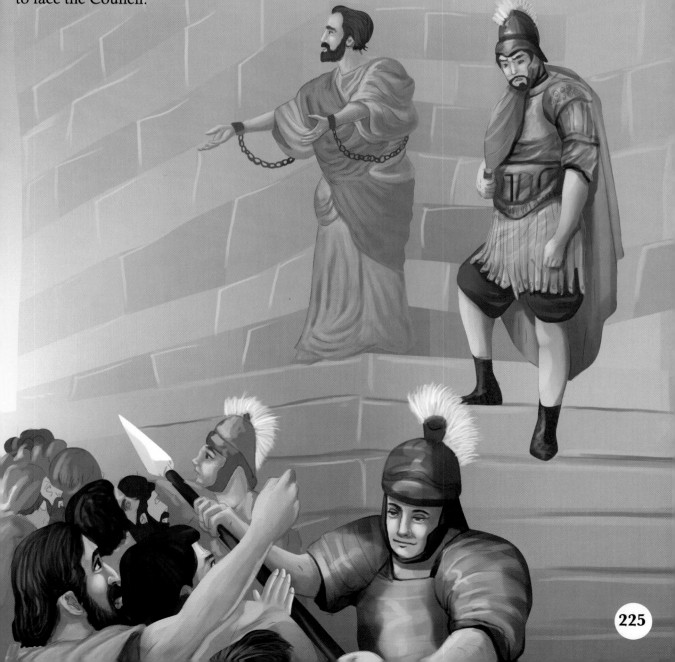

14 Paul is Saved

When Paul faced the council, they could not find any fault with him! The Jews plotted to kill him. Forty Jews took an oath not to eat nor drink till Paul was killed. Paul's sister's son heard their plan! He went to the castle where Paul was imprisoned and told him.

Paul told a centurion, "Take him to the tribune, Claudius Lysias." When the tribune questioned him, the boy revealed the Jews' plan. Lysias called two centurions and ordered two hundred soldiers, with seventy horsemen and two hundred spearmen, to take Paul safely to Felix, the governor.

Lysias wrote a letter to Felix, explaining that Paul was seized by the Jews over some issue with Jewish law that was not worthy of death! Felix read the letter. He commanded that Paul be kept in Herod's Judgement Hall until the Jews who accused him arrived.

15 Paul in Caesarea

After five days, the high priest Ananias and Jewish elders presented their case against Paul. They said that Paul was the ringleader of the Nazarene sect and was causing confusion among the Jews. The governor asked Paul to defend himself.

Commending Felix for judging the people for many years, Paul said that just twelve days earlier he had gone to worship in the temple in Jerusalem. No one found any fault with him then nor did they see him creating any trouble in the Synagogues or city. Paul stated his belief in the Jewish law and how Jesus fulfilled the law by His death and resurrection. Felix postponed giving his judgement until Lysias, the tribune, also came.

Felix later sent for Paul. While reasoning with him about righteousness and self-control, he came to know about God's coming judgement which made Felix trembled in fear.

16 Paul Before Festus

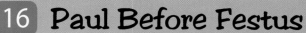
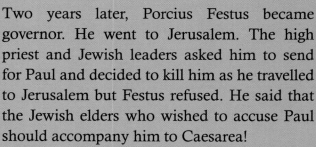

Two years later, Porcius Festus became governor. He went to Jerusalem. The high priest and Jewish leaders asked him to send for Paul and decided to kill him as he travelled to Jerusalem but Festus refused. He said that the Jewish elders who wished to accuse Paul should accompany him to Caesarea!

After Festus returned, he summoned Paul before the judgement seat. The Jews from Jerusalem accused Paul of doing terrible things, but they could not prove anything!

Paul replied that he had done nothing wrong. Festus, trying to please the Jews, asked Paul if he would go to Jerusalem. Paul said since he had offended neither the Jewish law nor the Roman law, and no one could prove his guilt, he would like to appeal to Caesar.

Festus consulted the Council and agreed.

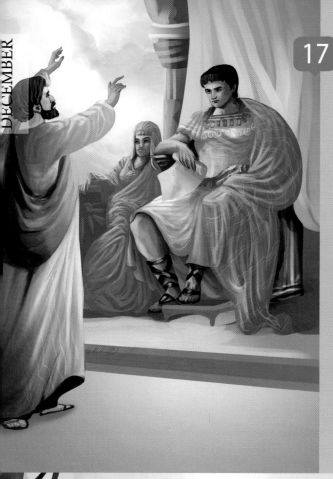

17 Paul and King Agrippa

Governor Festus requested King Agrippa to examine Paul. At the hall of hearing, Paul said that he was raised a Pharisee of the strictest sect. When he heard Christians preaching about Jesus of Nazareth, His death and resurrection, he was furious. Paul described how he persecuted the Christians for spreading a wrong doctrine. Paul narrated how Jesus met him on the Damascus road and Paul changed. The angry Jews now sought to kill him. Agrippa exclaimed. "Much learning has made you mad, Paul!"

Paul told Agrippa that he only preached what Moses and the prophets had foretold. Paul knew that Agrippa believed the prophets! "You almost persuade me to become a Christian, Paul," Agrippa replied. "I wish all men would do so!" said Paul. Agrippa declared that Paul could have been freed if he had not appealed to Caesar.

18 Paul Sails for Rome

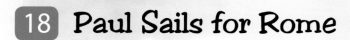

As Paul had appealed to Caesar, he had to go to Rome for trial. Julius, a centurion of Augustus's band, was put in charge of Paul and other prisoners.

Julius treated Paul kindly. Paul's friends, Luke and Aristarchus, accompanied him. They set sail from Adramyttium in Mysia along the western coasts of Asia Minor.

The next day, they reached Sidon. Julius allowed Paul to visit friends. They sailed across the northeast portion of the Mediterranean, passing Cyprus, to the southern coast of Asia Minor, and westward, past Cilicia and Pamphylia, and reached Myra in Lycia.

Now, they changed ships. Julius transferred Paul and the others on to a ship sailing in from Alexandria. Bad weather slowed them. With great difficulty, they reached Cnidus. Then, crossing Crete, they sailed through rough weather until they reached Fair Havens, a harbour near Lasea.

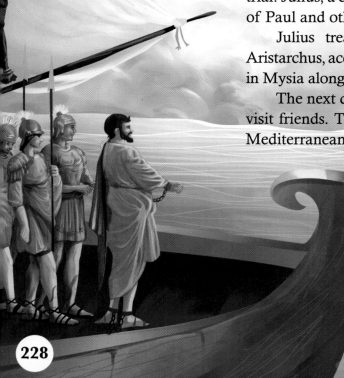

19 Storm at the Sea

The voyage became dangerous. The feast of the Day of Atonement was over. Paul warned the centurion of losing both cargo and ship if they continued but he did not listen. As Fair Havens was unsuitable during winter, they decided to sail to Phoenix in Crete.

But as they sailed westward, Euroclydon, a strong wind from the cliffs, struck them. Unable to steer, the ship was driven by the storm, till they reached Clauda. They struggled to hoist the small boat they had been towing, and secured the ship with cables to prevent it from being smashed apart.

The storm mercilessly tossed the ship. They dumped the cargo to lighten the ship and threw the ship's tackle overboard. With no sight of the sun or stars to get their bearings, they helplessly tossed, with no sign of land. All hope was abandoned.

20 Paul Gives Hope

The storm continued to rage and everyone aboard lost all hope. They were hungry, cold, wet and tired. Paul simply took command. He said, "Men, you should have listened to me when I warned you not to set sail from Crete. We have incurred loss. I urge you, be encouraged. I assure you that there will be no loss of life. The ship will be lost."

Paul told them how that very night an Angel of the God whom he served and worshipped, had appeared to him. The Angel had told Paul not to be afraid for he had to meet Caesar and face his trial. He also promised that God would spare the lives of all those on board. Paul encouraged them because he had faith in God that everything would happen exactly as he had been told, even though they would soon be shipwrecked on an island.

229

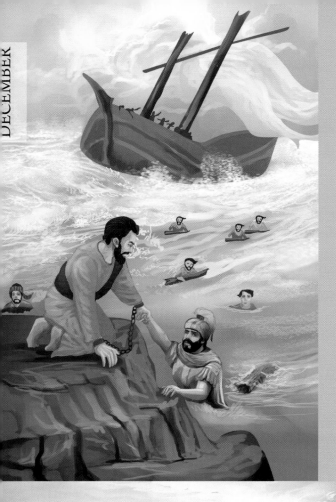

21 Shipwrecked!

After fourteen days, at midnight, the sailors felt that land was near. A reading showed ocean depth of 120 feet. Afraid that the ship would hit the rocks, they let down four anchors.

The sailors planned to escape from the ship in a small boat. Paul sensed this and told the centurion that unless everyone remained aboard, no one would be saved. The soldiers then cut the ropes letting the boat adrift.

At dawn, Paul encouraged the men to eat. He himself prayed and ate bread. They noticed a bay with a beach and planned to land.

They struck a reef and the ship ran aground. The stern started cracking. The soldiers wanted to kill the prisoners, but the centurion stopped them! He wanted to save Paul. He ordered everyone to jump overboard, float on the broken planks and reach the shore. Finally, everyone landed safely just as Paul had said.

22 Paul in Malta

They had landed on the island of Malta. It was cold and rainy! The natives lighted a fire to warm them. A poisonous viper came out, bit Paul and clung to his hand. Paul shook the snake off his hand! It fell into the fire. He was not harmed at all. The natives waited for Paul to die. When Paul remained healthy, they called him a God!

Publius, the Island Chief, and a wealthy landowner, had graciously welcomed and hosted them for three days. His father was suffering with fever and dysentery. Paul visited him and laid hands on him and prayed. He was healed. For the next three months, Paul prayed for and healed all the sick people on the island.

Gratefully, the natives honoured the ship's company, providing them all their requirements to continue their journey to Rome.

23 Paul Reaches Rome

After waiting for three months in Malta, the ship's company decided to leave for Rome. They all boarded an Alexandrian ship. It carried the figurehead of the Twin Brothers, Castor and Pollux, believed to be the patron Gods of sailors! They sailed to Puteoli.

News reached the Christians in Rome that Paul was in Puteoli. Two groups of eager believers set out to meet him. One group travelled 43 miles to the Market of Appius and the other travelled 33 miles to the Three Taverns. Paul stayed with them for seven days enjoying their fellowship, care and love. Paul thanked God for them. He was strengthened in his faith, for he did not know what awaited him when he faced Caesar. When Paul finally reached Rome he was given a house to live by himself, with a soldier to guard him.

24 Paul Meets the Jews of Rome

Paul invited the Roman Jewish leaders home. They did not know why Paul was brought to Rome but they wanted to know about the Christian faith that Paul preached.

So, Paul explained to them, that though he had done nothing against the Jews or Jewish customs, yet he had been delivered as a prisoner. They wanted to free him because there was no cause worthy of death. But Paul explained that because the Jews had so strongly objected, he appealed to Caesar.

The Jews started visiting Paul. Some believed Paul but others rejected him. Paul sadly said, "The Holy Spirit rightly said through Isaiah, the prophet, go to these people who will hear but never understand." Paul lived in Rome for two years preaching about Jesus.

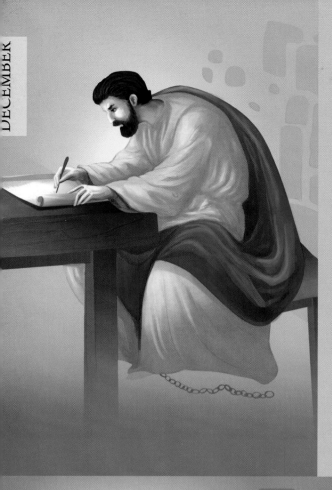

25 Return of the Runaway Slave

Paul wrote a touching letter to Philemon, who had become a Christian after hearing Paul preach. The church met in his home, so Paul commended him for his faith and good work.

Once Philemon's slave, Onesimus had run away and met Paul. Later he became a Christian. He began to help Paul so much that Paul had adopted him as his son. Paul was sending Onesimus back to Philemon and reassured him that Onesimus would be very helpful. Paul now requested that Philemon take back Onesimus forever, no longer as a slave, but as a beloved brother in the Lord.

Paul asked Philemon to receive Onesimus back into his household like he was receiving Paul, himself. Paul also offered to pay for anything Onesimus owed to Philemon. Paul was confident that Philemon would consent.

26 Paul and Epaphroditus

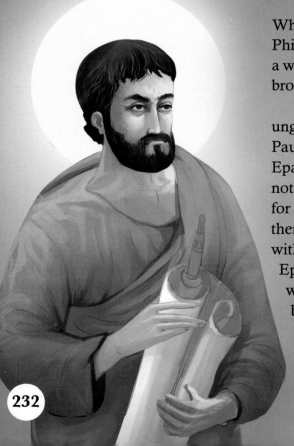

When Paul was imprisoned in Rome, the church at Philippi sent Epaphroditus to help him. He became such a wonderful companion to Paul that Paul called him, 'my brother', 'my fellow worker', and 'my fellow soldier'!

Epaphroditus looked after Paul's needs ungrudgingly. When Epaphroditus had come to help Paul, he had travelled 700 miles and had fallen ill. Epaphroditus was concerned that the believers should not hear of his illness; otherwise, they would feel sorry for having sent him! He was more concerned about them than he was about himself. After that he stayed with Paul and recovered. Paul felt that God had healed Epaphroditus to lessen Paul's own burdens! Now Paul was sending Epaphroditus back to Philippi, where the believers were waiting for news.

Though Paul's death is not recorded in the Bible, history records that this wonderful, tireless Apostle of the gospel was freed, re-imprisoned and finally killed.

27 Letter from James

Besides the four gospels, the New Testament contains several letters written by the Apostles and believers in Christ to the different churches.

The Lord Jesus was born of the Holy Spirit overshadowing Mary. Matthew, Jesus's disciple records in his gospel that later Mary and Joseph were blessed with other children. James, one of them, wrote this letter to the Christians.

James and the other children never believed in Jesus when He was preaching. But after Jesus's death and resurrection, James became His devoted follower, a respected member of the church at Jerusalem and was called James, the Just.

James saw the Jewish Christians slipping in their faith and encouraged them to ask God for wisdom. His work was to show faith in action, "for faith without work is dead."

He spoke of controlling one's tongue, as loose speech can cause untold damage. Finally, he urged them to pray at all times.

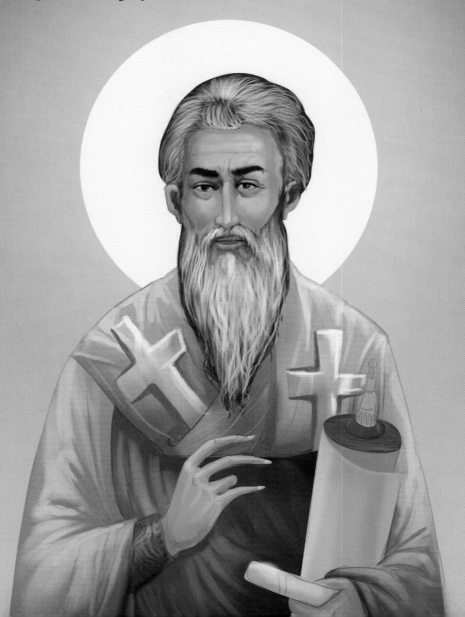

28 Letters from Peter

Peter, a fisherman, was one of Jesus's first disciples. Peter was called to preach to the Jews that Jesus was the way to God, because He was the Messiah of whom the prophets had foretold.

Peter learnt that Jesus had come to save all men, not just the Jews, so, in his letters to the Christians, he encouraged both the Jews and gentiles. In his first letter, Peter encourages the Christians to understand their privileges, duties, relationships and responsibilities to God, their country, and those within and outside the church. He highlights the suffering and service that a believer must endure for Christ's sake.

Peter's second letter warns Christians of false teachers influencing the church. He encourages believers to develop strong characteristics like faith, courage, knowledge, patience, godliness, brotherly kindness, hospitality and love.

29 Faithful to the End

Caesar Domitian had exiled John, Jesus's faithful disciple, to the small island of Patmos, near Ephesus. On the Lord's day, as John was praying, he heard a voice, "I am the First and the Last. Write what you see and send it to the seven churches in Asia."

The seven churches are Ephesus, Smyrna, Pergamos, Thyatira, Sardis, Philadelphia and Laodicea. They are in Modern Turkey. Satan was attacking the young churches with false teachers, religious persecution and spiritual decline. Through 'Revelation', God encouraged the churches to endure suffering, repent and renew themselves spiritually by following His Word, assuring them of eternal hope and victory over Satan through Christ Jesus.

Revelation reveals the Tribulation that the world must face, and the Triumphal return of Christ for the church.

30 The Heavenly City

Jesus declared that He is the Way, the Truth and the Life. He promised to take the believers to be with them forever. An Angel explained about Heaven to John in his vision. No sun or moon will be required, for the glory of God is its brightness. The length, breadth and height of the Heavenly city are equal. The city itself is made of pure gold, but transparent like clear glass. The city wall is made of Jasper. The city's twelve foundation layers are made of precious stones. There are twelve gates, each made of a single pearl, with an Angel at each gate.

The crystal clear River of Life flows from the throne of God. The Tree of Life produces twelve kinds of fruit, none of them forbidden! The leaves are for the healing of the nations. No illness, pain or tears can ever exist there.

31 All Those who Trust Christ

The Bible asserts that it is written for a man to be born once and to die once—with no exceptions! But, there is a second death, a permanent separation from God! The Lord Jesus is the Resurrection and Life. Whoever believes in Jesus and follows His teachings shall escape eternal death and the Lake of Fire.

Every Christian will live in Heaven. Their names are recorded in the Book of Life. Jesus promised to return for His Church. His return will be sudden, unannounced and unexpected. The Lord Jesus will reward every Christian according to his works with Crowns of Righteousness, Glory and Life! The Bible closes with those glorious words, "He which testifieth these things saith, Surely I come quickly. Amen. Even so, come, Lord Jesus!"

OTHER TITLES IN THIS SERIES

ISBN: 978-93-84225-31-5

ISBN: 978-81-87107-53-8

ISBN: 978-81-87107-55-2

ISBN: 978-81-87107-52-1

ISBN: 978-93-80069-35-7

ISBN: 978-93-80070-84-1

ISBN: 978-93-80070-83-4

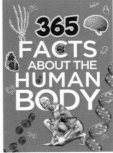
ISBN: 978-93-84625-93-1

ISBN: 978-93-83202-81-2

ISBN: 978-93-80070-79-7

ISBN: 978-93-84625-92-4

ISBN: 978-93-85031-29-8

ISBN: 978-93-84225-33-9

ISBN: 978-93-84225-32-2

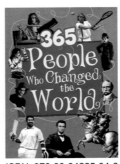
ISBN: 978-93-84225-34-6

ISBN: 978-81-87107-56-9

ISBN: 978-93-81607-49-7

ISBN: 978-81-87107-58-3

ISBN: 978-81-87107-57-6

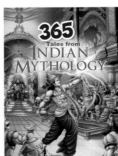
ISBN: 978-81-87107-46-0